PRAISE FOR

Sexy ... it's not that serious: How ⟨barcode⟩ *nd size*

"Morgan Toombs is a maste⟨barcode⟩nd spirit of your own unique de⟨barcode⟩*ot That* *Serious* she shares wisdom ga⟨barcode⟩ ...u shows how when you learn ways to s ...g unhappy with your body and start owning your authentic sexy, as defined by you, life takes on a brilliant new direction. Beneath and between her words we can hear a calling of greater confidence that leads to healthier relationships, more success, and even expanded financial prosperity. This is the real gift of this wonderful book."

— Marsh Engle
Author of The Six Essentials: Where Power, Passion, and Purpose Connects
Host of The Marsh Engle Show on CBS Radio

"I absolutely LOVE this book!!! It is fun, playful, powerfully healing and brilliantly written! It engages the reader continuously throughout, taking us on a journey of new sexy and feeling acceptance on every level! I want to jump up and down and share this book with the world! ... this work will truly transform your life in a powerfully positive direction.

— Tara Antler
Author of books: The Heart of Flourishing & The Healing Manual
Host of The Heart of Flourishing Radio Show

"Morgan's book is a giant leap in the forward movement of self-worth for the mothers and daughters of the world. Thank you, Morgan, for all your efforts to awaken the women of the 21st century!"

— Mindy Cowen
Founder and Director of Mothering Ministries

"I am so excited for and about this book. Everyday, across the globe, there are women of all ages who struggle with body image and self esteem as it relates to how they look and perceive others to see them. This book should be the next present you get for the women in your life be they your mother, sister, aunt, grandma, daughter or friend."

- Juannittah Kamera, RN, MScHPPH, MRSPH
Health Promotion Programs Coordinator - Student Health and Wellness
Ryerson University

"This is a book that will have you smiling right from the start! Morgan has taken a topic that can be incredibly controversial and uncomfortable and turned it into something fun. Light-hearted and playful, Sexy...It's Not That Serious will give you a powerful shift in understanding your own sense of what it is to feel sexy. Morgan's work gives women of all ages a powerful call to be authentic and to feel beautiful in their own skins. I loved it from start to finish! A definite must read for 2013."

- Andrea Ivanka
Speaker, Consultant
Author of Get UNSTUCK. 5 Steps to Freedom. One Woman's Inspiring Story
from Tragedy to Triumph

In this groundbreaking book *Sexy ... It's Not That Serious: How To Feel Sexy At Any Age And Size* a powerful offering is made to women around the globe: a safe bridge for them to cross into the confidence and strength that is their femininity. Morgan Toombs is a master at weaving together research, cultural examples, as well as lived experiences to help guide you, the reader, as you step into the most beautiful and radiant expression of yourself."

- Josephine Auciello
Femminine Essence Coach
Co-Author of Inspirational Strategies for an Audaciously Authentic Life

SEXY ...
IT'S NOT *THAT* SERIOUS
How to feel sexy at any age and size

Morgan B Toombs, BScN. (hons)
@morgan_toombs

THE VIBRANT YOU TRAINING INSTITUTE INC.

To order additional books or to buy in bulk, please call our Special Markets Department at 1-855-8-UR-SEXY

To request author information, or for speaker or other media requests, contact Media Relations at 1-855-8-UR-SEXY

Published by:
The Vibrant You Training Institute Inc.
c/o The Centre for Social Innovation
215 Spadina Ave, Suite 400, Toronto, Ontario, M5T 2C7

ISBN 978-0-9917577-0-1

Toombs, Morgan B, 1979-
Sexy ... it's not that serious: How to feel sexy at any age and size / Morgan Toombs
1. Women's Health. 2. Self-actualization (psychology). 3. Esteem. 4. Sexuality. 5. Empowerment. I. Morgan Toombs II. Title.

First Printing 2013
Printed and bound in the United States

Copy Editor Primary: Tanja So
Copy Editor Secondary: Samantha Haas
Jacket Design: Alexander VonNess
Photography: Nadia Pejic

DISCLAIMER

The information provided in this book has been selected to provide helpful information on the subjects discussed. However, it cannot replace or substitute for the services of trained professionals in any field, including, but not limited to medical and psychological health. In particular, you should regularly consult your personal physician in all matters relating to physical and/or mental health, particularly concerning any symptoms that may require diagnosis or medical attention.

The research in this book was obtained from reliable sources and the author and publisher made every effort to ensure that the information in this book was correct at press time. However, in view of the possibility of human error, neither the author nor any other party who was involved in the preparation or publication of this work warrants that the information contained herein is in every respect accurate or complete, and therefore does not assume and hereby disclaims any liability to any party for any loss, damage, or disruption caused by errors or omissions, whether such errors or omissions result from negligence, accident, or any other cause.

The publisher and author make no representations or warranties concerning any action, exercise or experience by any person following the information or activities provided within this book. Neither the publisher nor the author will be liable for any direct, indirect, consequential, special, exemplary or other damages that may result from your engagement with the content, including but not limited to injury or illness. You alone are responsible and accountable for your decisions, actions and results in life. By choosing to read this book, you agree not to attempt to hold the author, publisher or any other party who took part in creating this book liable for any such decisions, actions or results, at any time, under any circumstance.

The personal accounts are based on the lived experience of the author and do not take into consideration any other point of view. Therefore, no person within this book is to be inferred as an accurate or actual representation of any person - living or dead. All of the case studies have been altered to protect the identity and confidential information of clients. Any resemblance to any person, coaching session or event, is purely coincidental.

GIVING BACK

A percentage of global sales will be donated to
Because I Am A Girl
in order to positively impact the lives of
women and girls globally.

DEDICATION

To my mom, for reinforcing within me the REALity that it is, in fact, safe to live outside "the box."

To the love of my life, Jerome (Jeromeo) Robins. The anchor of your love makes my life tremendously delicious.

To Ingrid (Kittenhouse) Kittlaus, for loving me enough to tell me the truth. Without you, this book would not have been written.

To my grandparents, Gordon and Mary Toombs. Thank you for awakening me to the possibility that I too can pioneer change within the realm of sexuality.

ACKNOWLEDGMENTS

I am deeply grateful to so many people for their love, guidance, support and kindness while this book was being created. Specifically:

My partner - Jerome Robins. Thank you for being so supportive and loving. I appreciate how you encourage me to chase my dreams and then celebrate with me when I reach them. I love you.

Margareth Zanchetta, you're an extraordinary nursing instructor (and human being!) whose feedback and perspective for this book were invaluable. Thank you!

The "Dream Team": Kelsey Lammers, Tanja So, Samantha Haas, Nadia Pejic, and Alexander VonNess. You are all so talented! Thank you for being so good at what you do. Your skills and efforts helped make this book what it is.

My beta readers: Jenni Alerton, Todd Banks, Ildiko Hegyi, Jonathan Slade, Jackie Tinkler, Viviana Medel, Heather Thomas and Melissa Spence. Thank you so much for your willingness to look upon my work-in-progress. Your honest feedback was both heard and incorporated.

Finally, thank you to my personal cheerleading team: Natalia Popovich, Mickey Cirak, Ryan (the Delectable Mr.) Kennedy, Jordan Lee, Sirena Liladrie, Jen Carter, Vanessa Reid, Tanja Yardley, Naomi Low, Barbara Toombs, Ingrid Kittlaus, Susan Wagner, Pamela Putman, Tara Antler, Marsh Engle, Donna DeLuca, Signe Nessing, Amandine Bachman, Chantal Labine, Christine Ebadi, Carol Hamilton Niusha Barmala, and Misty Tripoli. I am sorry if I have forgotten anyone. Thank you for believing in me. I love you all.

CONTENTS

A NOTE TO READERS

Hello Beautiful … Morgan here.

First of all, I'd like to thank you for taking time out of your busy day to be here with me.

Secondly, I'd like to congratulate you for opening this book. It takes courage to explore the possibility of experiencing NEW levels of confidence and personal power. Therefore, I celebrate YOU and all of your **deliciousness**!

I imagine you are wondering why you should read this book and/ or what makes me the expert on **sexy**. Below are the answers to those questions, as well as the history regarding why this book was created:

- I am a pioneering expert in the concept of Authentic Sexy and have been researching this book for over a decade.
- For more than 13 years, I have had the privilege of being a sensual movement expert (both an instructor and professional dancer), which has granted me a unique opportunity to view women "naked" (in their vulnerability) as they experienced how safe it can be for them to authentically express their beautiful sensuality in ways that honor them. This book is my way to **Pay It Forward**; to offer that same opportunity to other women who are ready to step into their human right and feel sexy, in their own ways and on their own terms.
- My background also includes being high level fitness professional (meaning an both international fitness presenter and

trainer/certifier of budding fitness professionals). It was in the fitness world that I learned that most women are ashamed about the size, shape, weight and beauty of their bodies.

- Those two aforementioned experiences were why I chose to earn a Bachelor of Science degree with honors in nursing. It was my goal to become this generation's **Sue Johanson**. However, instead of talking about sex toys and sexual play, I wanted to talk about components of sexuality that are not commonly talked about - *even though* they can powerfully impact a woman's health. Specifically, how a woman's esteem, confidence, and body image, as well as her engagement with life and other women can be profoundly impacted *if she feels* she does not embody the socially constructed vision of "sexy" (beauty, youthfulness and/or body size). Why? Because even though it is the twenty first century, a woman is *still* subtly taught that her social worth is anchored to her physicality.

- In 2009 I was awarded a humanitarian award for my work with women and mental health. That level of compassion is the energy from which this book was written. My background has made me aware that "holding space" for women to experience life on their own terms is considerably more powerful than trying to "fix" them. After all, they are not broken. Instead, it's the outdated and damaging views our society maintains that are broken.

- The idea for this book was born from the frustration that came as a result of an aggressive, internal and seemingly never ending battle that I waged against my body; one that made me feel like no matter what I did, I was never quite "good enough." I was certain that there was another way, so I began to investigate. I explored academic research, as well as other womens' experiences of how they felt about their bodies, body image and pressures to embody our society's vision of sexy, and realized that most women were feeling the exact same way I was! With that realization I made the

commitment to figure out a way to inspire women –
regardless of their age, weight, beauty, or body size –
discover a NEW expression of sexy that not only nourishes
them, but also helps them step into a new relationship with
their bodies and, in turn, their lives.

- To be clear, this book is meant to shift the old paradigm
  of sexy - western society's standard definition of feminine
  beauty and desirability - into a NEW definition of sexy:
  authentic sexy. This new paradigm of authentic sexy is not
  "just" about being sexy externally. It's about how you engage
  with life; how you view your body. It's also about learning
  how to embrace your exquisite and **beautiful** nature, as you
  are, right now.

- Both the implicit and explicit messaging of this book are
  tied to a global movement that is happening. Specifically,
  social progress has made it possible for a woman's worth to
  no longer be based solely on her age, beauty, sexuality and/
  or body size. However, there are multiple indicators identi-
  fying a gap between women *thinking* these aforementioned
  points and *embodying* that thinking. This book offers a
  solution to that problem. In fact, it is my hope that this
  book will awaken women to the reality that if we don't take
  action immediately, these same pressures related to body,
  beauty, esteem and sexy will continue to profoundly impact
  the lives *and health* of future generations.

- The design and word choices of this book have been
  selected to reflect an easy and accessible method for
  individual self discovery. Specifically, I have included
  exercises within the chapters that have been designed to
  support the examination of your conscious (and unconscious) beliefs so that you can feel free enough to shine
  your **authentic**, beautiful light to the world – in your own
  way and on your own terms.

- You are welcome to read this book in whatever way serves
  you: from cover to cover, one chapter at a time, or even
  by selecting random FUNdamental truths, exercises or

lessons to explore and/or engage. Just like expressions of authentic sexy, there is no right or wrong way to read this book.

- Please note: the glossary has been included at the opening of the book in order to familiarize you with the language that will be used during this **book experience**. The words within the glossary have been purposely identified and/or reassigned alternate meanings in order to help you re-frame your view of sexy.

Alright, Beautiful. There you have it. If you are ready to learn how to tap into deeper feelings of confidence, esteem and, of course, SEXY, please continue reading. There are countless delicious treasures inside this book for you to unearth.

Enjoy!

Morgan Toombs

GLOSSARY

---

*Definitions for **bold-typed**
words and expressions can be found in
this glossary. To avoid visual distraction,
each word will be bold-typed within the
text once, even if it appears numerous times.*

Alive – Awake. Present. Looking out at the world through your two eyes. Feeling vibrant inside your incredible **meat suit**.

Animate/Animation – To bring to life. Making your body move in animated ways (versus in "cardboard" or boring ways).

Armor – A protection mechanism. Can be emotional, physical, psychological and/or sexual.

Authentic – Real. Genuine. True to one's honest *self*.

Authentic sexy – 1) The NEW confident power among women. Reflections of authentic sexy are as unique as the individual expressing it. An expression of humanity that is impossible to get wrong. 2) A redefined vision of sexy that fits each woman's age, curves, personality and life. 3) Being the authentic, feminine you. No pretensions. Emanating your beautiful and exquisite human energy. 4) A **way of being** that is rooted in love versus the historically constructed vision of sexy, which is rooted in judgment and fear.

Authentic strength – Authentic vulnerability. A woman's *true* strength.

Awake – Refers to being alive and truly living life versus being on auto pilot or just going through the motions.

Synonyms – **present**, alive, conscious, aware.

Be/Being – 1) A state of presence. To be in the now. 2) Another way to express the culmination of the experience of being human (i.e. a joyful/sensual/spiritual being).

Beauty/Beautiful – A joyful lightness that emanates from every cell in your body. Authentic beauty is accessible to all women - regardless of their age, background or body size - and exists in an abundant supply.

Beautiful body – A reference that honors a person's beautiful meat suit – regardless of size, shape, color, etc.

Book experience – An experience opportunity brought forth by reading a book - should you choose to engage the content in meaningful ways.

Bold-typed – An example of how words within the text will be identified. These words will be listed within the glossary.

Box - A constructed perception of how things are. A "box" view can seem fixed even though it is, in fact, changeable. This concept is related to the concept of **status quo.**

Dance your life – Moving to the currents of your life in ways that feel good to you. You can only do this when you are **awake.**

Delicious/Deliciousness – The total of all your love, beauty, goodness, sweetness and sexiness in motion.

Dirty – A judgment term that views sexuality and the body's sensual expression of this as negative or bad. It is grounded in outdated views of sexuality but has yet to leave our common language.

Disordered eating – Non-health based pattern of eating.

DNA/Cellular level – A truth that your being understands right to the core of every cell. A previously unconscious notion that, after awakening to it, becomes an integrated aspect of your being that is so familiar to you that its Truth becomes embedded in your cells; embedded in your DNA.

Ego – A frame of reference that identities with non-heart centered experiences and/or objects.

En-JOY – The quality of experiencing life as joy. It is only possible to experience this when living in the present moment.

Freak flag – The unique identifier of your delicious and playful world. The world only you can see. Your freak flag encompasses your views and passions as well as your completely delicious and unabashed beautiful nature.

Gospel – According to Dictionary.com, "Absolute truth." According to the author, a status quo that should be looked at critically before accepting.

Hat(s) – Another way to frame the concept of "role." Example: Sometimes she wears the hats of mother, wife, CEO and sensual woman within one day.

Heart light - The beautiful, love filled brightness that emanates from an authentic **human being**.

Heart song – One's authentic **YES!** What makes one "come alive." What nourishes a person and facilitates a joyful and vibrant life.

Herd mentality – An uncritical following of the status quo; following blindly as if a sheep.

Human being – An **awake** individual. One who is conscious and aware.

Inappropriate – A judgment term, "bad." Being judgmental separates a person from the situation, which renders them not present and therefore they relinquish their power.

Interpersonal fail – Unsuccessful interaction between two or more people.

Juicy – Full of feminine **yum**. Fluidly sexy, beautiful and gorgeous. Can also refer to feminine genital wetness. However, this context is not used within this book.

Mask – An inauthentic place where a person can choose to hide their authentic self. Example: A title or an identity like "good girl."

Meat suit – Your incredible, physical human body. The structure that supports your bones, organs and creates attachments for movement to occur. Coined by Misty Tripoli. (http://www.mistytripoli.com)

On reserve attitude – A method of hiding your authentic self behind the mask of a role or perceived role.

Own/Owning – Confidently standing in, accepting, and embracing all of the deliciousness that you are.

Pay(ing) it forward – Sharing and facilitating growth for others, which results from profound growth one has personally experienced.

Perfect imperfection(s) – One may perceive oneself as "flawed." However, it is these flaws that make the individual unique and "perfect." If the person did not have the perceived flaws then they would not be who they are, thus perfect imperfection.

Present – In the moment. In the "now." You are aware and simply being.

Programming – Learned social scripts and ways of being often taught by institutions like: family, schools, government, the church, peer groups and more. Status quo s are examples of commonly held social programming.

REALity – Synonymous with **Truth**. The real experience underneath the illusion. REALity is accessible if one remains present and anchored in the now.

Real you – The authentic you, without **armor**.

Real them – The authentic and true them.

Safe – An emotionally secure place from which to engage with the world. A safe place allows people to open up and share their authentic selves.

Sensual groove – A unique and delicious way of engaging the world by dancing one's life and/or body. This occurs by choosing for oneself what feels good regarding your sensuality, sexiness, body, abilities and more.

Sensual whiplash - A neck injury resultant of doing inauthentic or disconnected sensual movement. This problem can be avoided by going inside your body during sensual movement and authentically animating the movement versus doing the move with the intention to look good/sexy, copy someone else, or "get it right."

Sexy - According to Dictionary.com: Risque, radiating sexuality and/or glamorous.

According to the author: 1) A blurry concept that needs to be re-defined so that it fits each person expressing it. 2) For the purposes of this book - a culturally constructed status quo that is unrealistic and biologically unachievable for the majority of women in this society. A powerful, yet inconspicuous, pressure that profoundly impacts women of all ages due to women feeling the need to present themselves as young, fit and beautiful in order to have social value and visibility.

Sexy Sister – A woman who makes no apologies for being gorgeous – inside and out. She claims her space in this world and expresses herself however she pleases – side stepping social expectations, scripts and/or sexy definitions that do not come in her size, shape, style or color. She defines for herself what sexy means, how it dresses and what kind of swagger it displays. She knows, right down to
her DNA – that she is exquisite, unrepeatable, and 100% **delicious.**

Shackles – Ties to ways of thinking and/or being that do not serve the individual. Oftentimes they are habits and/or patterns that the individual does not realize they have control over. Individual's have the power to unbind themselves from shackles. The keys are education, desire and effort.

Slut – According to Dictionary.com: "An immoral woman."

The author's definition: A judgment term that has the power to bind sexual authenticity and stunt a woman's sexual, psychological and social growth. For example, a young woman who was called a slut as a teen might work really hard to NOT be perceived as a slut and thus ends up adopting the role of a "good girl." Or, people who are scared of being viewed as a slut because of the social implications it may have on a woman's sense of self, esteem and more. Or, some women who are viewed as sluts may embody the label and play out the role, disconnecting themselves from their authentic, empowered and joyful expression of sexuality.

Status quo – A socially determined "usual" or "typical" way of doing things. Example: The current status quo for female expressions of sexy is confusing and outdated.

"Strong" vs Strong – A **mask** of strength versus true, vulnerable strength.

Sue Johanson – A pioneer in sexual health education in Canada. (http://www.talksexwithsue.com)

Tent – Hide.

True sexy – Synonymous with authentic sexy. An authentic expression of sexy, as defined by the individual for the individual. A new and empowering frame of sexy that boosts an individual's confidence, esteem, personal power and perception of self.

Truth – **REALity.** Cellular level "knowing." There are some fundamental, universal truths that are true for all of mankind. There are also individual truths that are true for one individual that may or may not be true for another.

UNlearn – The act of unprogramming and/or unlearning. In the context of this book, it is important for readers to give themselves space to learn new ways of engaging with the world and themselves in order to re-frame and redefine sexy to suit their age, curves, personality and life. UNlearning creates the space for new thoughts and REALities to set in.

Way(s) of being – How one is or acts. Ways one **animates** one's life.

YES! – Your Truth. Your unique and instinctual path that is determined by your heart. If you have the courage to listen to and follow your unique YES!, you will feel happier and your life will be filled with yum.

(You)nique – Each individual is unique. This spelling offers a visual play on this concept. Coined by Misty Tripoli. (http://www.mistytripoli.com)

Yum – The total of all your goodness. Positive feelings brought about by one's lived experience.

NOTES

gospel. (n.d.). Dictionary.com Unabridged. Retrieved from Dictionary.com website: http://dictionary.reference.com/browse/gospel

sexy. (n.d.). Dictionary.com Unabridged. Retrieved from Dictionary.com website: http://dictionary.reference.com/browse/sexy

slut. (n.d.). Dictionary.com Unabridged. Retrieved from Dictionary.com website: http://dictionary.reference.com/browse/slut

SEXY ...
IT'S NOT THAT SERIOUS
How to feel sexy at any age and size

INTRODUCTION

---

*Redefining Your Concept Of Sexy Is Vital To
Helping You Live A Vibrantly Happy Life.*

Today we are going to redefine the concept of sexy.

Why?

Because sexy is not that serious.

... It's also not what we think it is.

I realize that when you picked up this book you probably thought you would be opening another "how to" guide that would teach you how to be incredibly sexy like Rhianna, Carmen Electra, Sharron Stone or Sophia Loren.

Rest assured, you are correct ...

IF you are Rhianna, Ms. Electra, Ms. Stone or Ms. Loren.

However, if you are not one of these aforementioned women then I have to confess, I do not have a magic formula for turning you into someone you are not.

I do not have a wand.

I am not a fairy godmother.

You will not turn into a pumpkin at midnight.

However, what I CAN do is help you to peel away those silly layers that make you *think* you have to be (or look like) Rhianna, Ms. Electra, Ms. Stone or Ms. Loren to be considered sexy, delicious, worthy of attention, and/or worthy of love.

This book experience is designed to help you understand – on a **DNA/cellular level** – that you, AS YOU, are sexier and more delicious than a you that is pretending to be someone else.

Make sense?

Good.

The main concept of this book is that sexy is not *that* serious.

However, there are plenty of messages out there (read: within media and our culture) that try to impress upon us that it is.

In fact, sexy appears to be a very serious and important part of a woman's life because it is constantly reinforced by a hyper-bombardment of media messages that set the expectation for all women to be (or remain) young, thin and beautiful if they want to be desired and/or have social worth[1].

For clarity's sake, all of the aforementioned points are common components that comprise the contemporary norm of how a woman in this culture is expected to express sexy.

It it clear that *when she does* show up in her life this way, she is granted happiness, power, visibility and a myriad of other opportunities that can positively impact her quality of life[2].

Evidence of these "sexy expectations" - as well as both the pay off for embodying them and the price for not embodying them - can be found in countless

> "Art reflects our time, it is about our culture"
> *David Elliot*

advertisements, movies, television shows and song lyrics – to name but a few examples.

The sad truth is that these messages reflect outdated ways of thinking that have proven to bind women to the belief that their physical form is still a dominant barometer for their personal worth and thus their opportunities for happiness.

In fact, it is clear that many women still carry the burden of these outdated views with them into their lives.

Academic research indicates that when women internalize our society's beauty and body pressures then employ methods to embody the "perfect female form" their health can be seriously impacted[3].

Grounding the research within real life: after years of researching this topic, it is clear to me that women are suffering at the hands of an outdated and/or poorly defined concept of sexy.

In fact, it is apparent that regardless of age, marital status, parental status, dress size, external beauty and/or level of success and wealth – thousands of women are

Reality Check:
A 2012 research study explored how girls in their tweens (ages 10-12) view social worth, as related to beauty. The findings were remarkable. It is clear that both transmission of outdated social scripts and beauty embodying expectations for females within this culture are still occurring. Specifically, the girls recognized that a female's beauty is still the primary measure for how socially valuable she is perceived by others to be.[4] In other words, the more valuable a girl is perceived by her peers to be, the more opportunities she has for being included - which, oftentimes, can be directly related to her happiness and quality of life. The author would like to note that this isn't a small issue. These beliefs can be carried with a girl into her adult life and profoundly impact her experience and engagement with life.

experiencing the exact same thing ...

They don't feel sexy!

Why?

Because in this culture we have so many subtle rules and expectations attached to how a woman "is allowed" to express sexy - in order for her to NOT be seen as **inappropriate.**

For example, she needs to be mindful of:

her age,

where she is,

how she dresses,

social role expectations,

the time of day,

the social context/who's around,

as well as her attire, appearance and body size/shape - just to name a few examples.

Therefore, in addition to being confusing, all of these rules and expectations make expressing sexy really complicated.

As a result, **true sexy** - authentic, confidence boosting feminine expression - has been buried under a pile of expectations that are intangible, unachievable and even biologically unrealistic for the majority of women in this culture!

The truth is that I am not surprised that most women don't feel as delicious as they authentically are. The vision of sexy that they are trying to embody is both slippery and blurry. How can women expect to "get sexy right" - and feel good about themselves and their age/body/beauty - when the rules and expectations surrounding sexy continually shift?

The unfortunate effect of this phenomenon is that instead of trying to "figure it out" by sorting through the rubble of carelessly strewn sexy images and messages that communicate how women are "supposed to be," many women simply disconnect from being sexy.

In fact, my research indicates that most women either have no idea that sexy IS possible for them or they have forgotten how deliciously fun and nourishing embodying authentic sexy can be!

In some circles, sexy is even considered a **dirty** word!

This is why you will find women who look gorgeous externally but silently hate what they see in the mirror and wrestle with desperately low self esteem[5].

This is also why you will find so many women who don't connect to their authentic sexy because they have no idea what it is, where to start, or that it is accessible to them *even if* they have experienced certain life changes that traditionally yield them as "unsexy," such as menopause, motherhood, grand-motherhood, weight gain, divorce, etc.

However, what if I told you that when you *redefine sexy* so it becomes authentic to you and is based on *your* values, beliefs and body, you open yourself up to NEW levels of confidence and personal power?

---

5 Working within the glamour industry for over a decade exposed the author to reality of this. There are also several former professional models who are now sharing how they experienced their body, esteem and sense of self while modeling. Their musings are reflective of this statement (that they didn't feel gorgeous, even though their bodies were the physical expression of what gorgeous is supposed to look like in our society).

It's true!

In fact, redefining sexy demystifies it, which enables sexy to be what it is – both a life skill and a delicious expression that fits your age, curves, personality and life.

Additionally, when you redefine sexy to fit your unique specifications, not only do you realize that sexy is not *that* serious, you also find the key to so much that you have been searching for, such as:

improved relationships,

increased happiness,

increased confidence,

increased financial abundance,

increased success in your professional life,

increased sense of vibrancy and aliveness,

and/or deeper feelings of peace[6].

"How is that possible?" you ask.

It's simple.

Instead of *hiding*, you just allow yourself to **BE.**

In other words, instead of engaging in self defeating and unkind

dialogs or thoughts – about yourself and/or about others – you engage your life and "show up" as authentic, gorgeous, miraculous and unrepeatable you.

6 Based on testimonials from the author's clients and live event participants.

Furthermore, having the courage to step into this NEW expression of sexy that fits YOU unequivocally, you inadvertently have an amazing gift to pass on to your daughter(s).

Specifically, research indicates that young girls learn how to perceive and qualify their body and body image from their mothers[7].

This means that when you learn how to stop being unhappy with your body (age, beauty, weight, etc.) and start owning your authentic sexy, as defined by you, you can help protect the mental and emotional health of your female children!

And how timely considering all the bullying around the concept of sexy (i.e. name calling/bullying with words like "**slut**"[8]), contemporary industrial trends that target and sexualize child femininity[9], and the pressures our youth experience regarding "being sexy"[10].

How delicious if we, the adult mentors and role models for younger generations, can positively shape and impact their self perception so that they can learn what we already know – they are *already perfect*, as they are.

In fact, despite what they have been taught to understand - through both implicit and explicit cultural messaging - they don't need to "be sexy" (beautiful, etc.) in order to be liked or valued.

Why?

Because *not only* are they too young to be "sexy" but also because sexy is not that serious!

In fact, for them to be liked and valued, all they have to do is just be themselves.

---

10 During a conversation with an expert who educates grade school girls on esteem and body image, the author learned that girls commonly use the term "sexy" to refer to themselves and others. In fact, the term "sexy" is commonly used by kids today.

And guess what, my stunning **Sexy Sister**?

The same thing goes for you.

The fact of the matter is this: regardless of who you are, where you come from or what you have been taught, you cannot get sexy wrong ... no matter what you currently believe!

In fact, when sexy becomes authentic, you can only get it right!

I know it may sound like a bizarre concept.

However, it's the Truth.

It's also the truth that you opened this book for a reason.

You've been searching for something.

A message.

A sign.

Well, guess what, Sexy?

Today is your lucky day!

You have found the key that will unlock the door that will reveal the path to your authentic sexy, which means sexy as defined by you.

Are you, my Sexy Sister, ready to be hyper validated and seen for all the goodness that you are?

If so, I want you to know – from my heart to yours - that this book is my way to Pay It Forward so you can *also* realize how easy it is to let go of negative beliefs about your age, beauty, sexy and/or desirability so that you can finally wake up to *your* radiance and feel **safe** enough to embody the confident, sexy woman you innately are!

It is my intention that this book will give you the courage to find your own expression of authentic sexy – not only because it is such a delicious and nourishing aspect of life but also because there is no one else on this planet who can express your authentic sexy in exactly the way you do.

To sum up before we launch into Chapter 1:

Life.

This book.

They're not about being sexy.

Because sexy is not *that* serious!

Life and this book are really all about being.

You, my incredible, beautiful woman, are who I wrote this book for.

Sexy: A Life Skill

As a health educator, I recognize that "sexy" is a life skill.
It's true that sexy is not *that* serious. However, *it is
important* that everyone, men and women, feel sexy in
some way, shape or form if they want to attract a mate.
OK ... so maybe sexy *is* kind of serious.
Just not *that* serious.

The truth is, being authentically sexy doesn't have to be
complicated. In fact, when a person defines for themselves what sexy means - it becomes both impossible for
them to get wrong AND impossible for it to be bad!

It is because of this that sexy is no longer "scary" due to
the social repercussions it may have held.
For example: a woman being be vilified or ostracized by
other women for being explicitly sexy (meaning sexy in
a socially constructed, oftentimes perceptively negative
manner that changes based on a variety of factors).

Instead, sexy - when expressed authentically - becomes a
health boosting component of life that can help a woman
heal her relationship with her body simply because she
has learned that her age, weight, beauty and/or body size
ARE, in fact, "good enough," as they are; she doesn't have
to change a thing!

NOTES

1 Haas, C. F., Champion, A. & Secor, D. (2008). Motivating factors for seeking cosmetic surgery: A synthesis of the literature. *Plastic Surgical Nursing, 28(4),* p 177-182. Retrieved from ProQuest Nursing

2 Hurd Clarke, L & Griffin, M. (2008). Visible and invisible ageing: Beauty work as a response to ageism. *Aging & Society, 28,* 653-674. Retrieved from ProQuest Nursing

Hurd Clarke, L., Repta, R. & Griffin, M. (2007). Non-surgical cosmetic procedures: Older women's perceptions and experiences. *Journal of Women & Aging, 19(3/4),* p. 69-87. Retrieved from ProQuest Nursing

McCormick, M. L. (2008). Women's bodies aging: Culture, con text, and social work practice. *Journal of Women and Social Work, 23(4),* p 312-323. Retrieved from ProQuest Nursing

3 Bedford, J. L. & Johnson, C. S. (2006). Societal influences on body image dissatisfaction in younger and older women. *Journal of Women and Aging, 18(1),* p 41-55. Retrieved from ProQuest Nursing

Crerand, C. E., Infield, A. L. & Sarwer, D. B. (2007). Pyschological considerations in cosmetic breast augmentation. *Plastic Surgical Nursing, 27(3),* p 146-152. Retrieved from ProQuest Nursing

Haas, C. F., Champion, A. & Secor, D. (2008). Motivating factors for seeking cosmetic surgery: A synthesis of the literature. *Plastic Surgical Nursing, 28(4),* p 177-182. Retrieved from ProQuest Nursing

Hurd Clarke, L & Griffin, M. (2008). Visible and invisible ageing: Beauty work as a response to ageism. *Aging & Society, 28,* 653-674. Retrieved from ProQuest Nursing

Hurd Clarke, L., Repta, R. & Griffin, M. (2007). Non-surgical cosmetic procedures: Older women's perceptions and experiences. *Journal of Women & Aging, 19(3/4),* 69-87. Retrieved from ProQuest Nursing

McCormick, M. L. (2008). Women's bodies aging: Culture, con text, and social work practice. *Journal of Women and Social Work, 23(4),* 312-323. Retrieved from ProQuest Nursing

4 Collins, L. & Lidinsky, A. & Rusnock, A. & Torstrick, R.(2012). We're Not Barbie Girls: Tweens Transform a Feminine Icon. *Feminist Formations 24(1),* 102-126. The Johns Hopkins University Press. Retrieved from Project MUSE database

5 Comment found within a footnote in the text.

6 Comment found within a footnote in the text.

7 Zelman, K.M. (n.d.). The mother-daughter weight connection: Help your daughter have a healthy attitude about her weight. *Web MD.* http://www.webmd.com/healthy-beau ty/features/the-mother-daughter-weight-connection

8 Hodge, J. (October, 2012). Calling it 'bullying' doesn't do Amanda Todd justice. *The Huffington Post.* http://www. huffingtonpost.ca/jarrah-hodge/amanda-todd-bully ing-gender-slut-shaming_b_1964337.html

Sager, J. (October, 2012). Another suicide?! Slut shaming needs to stop. *Gurl.* http://www.gurl.com/2012/10/26/felicia-garcia-slut-shaming-suicide

9 American Psychological Association, Task Force on the Sexualization of Girls. (2010). Report of the APA Task Force on the Sexualization of Girls. Retrieved from http://www.apa.org/pi/women/programs/girls/report-full.pdf

10 Comment found within a footnote in the text.

"Life isn't about being sexy
... becuase sexy is not *that* serious!

Life is really all about being."

CHAPTER ONE
A revolution is brewing

*It Is Imperative That The Concept Of Sexy
Evolves Into An Empowering Feature Of Life.
Why? Because It Is Time For The Women And
Girls In This Culture To Stop Suffering.*

As we've already discussed, certain avenues within mainstream culture, such as pop music and numerous reality TV shows, ignore much of the progress we've achieved, as a culture, to move beyond defining women solely based on physical appearance.

Specifically, images that perpetuate a woman's worth as being synonymous with her ability to fit within the socially constructed vision of sexy[1]: young, thin and beautiful.

This is an issue because there is very little variance – in terms of shape, size, color and attractiveness – within the *positively viewed* female body images the media portrays.

This homogeneity of images does not reflect the vast majority of women in contemporary western society and sets the status quo for what a "normal" female body should look like at a level that very few women can ever achieve[2].

Thus, women of all ages, experience pressure to alter their bodies by way of dieting, exercise, plastic surgery, make up or any other means required to embody the "perfect" (or sexy) female form.

In fact, research indicates that women are largely dissatisfied with their bodies regardless of their age and/or normal weight status[3].

In other words, regardless of whether a woman is young or old, plump or thin, she likely doesn't feel as sexy, desirable and/or attractive as she would like to be.

This issue of "not feeling good enough" is widespread and impacts almost all women in this culture[4].

Methods Women Use To Embody "Sexy":
Diets[5],
Makeup[6],
Laxitives[7],
Hairstyles[6],
Fake nails[6],
Fitness regimes[5],
Botox injections[6],
Weight loss pills[7],
Binging/purgeing[7],
Nutritional supplements[5],
Waxing/shaving/plucking/lasering[6],
And various forms of plastic surgery[6] (liposuction, face lift, nose job, and breast augmentation, just to name a few examples).

These methods range from the common to the extreme and can be found in almost all women's lives. The ease with which many of these methods can be both attained and employed, combined with the views our society holds about *the necessity* of their use, leads many women to feeling less than good enough. Thus, they continue to engage in one or many body and/or beauty altering techniques which, in turn, perpetuates both the outdated status quo and this confidence and esteem damaging cycle.

---

4 There are multiple research studies on this topic. However, to ground the reality that this is actually a lived experience of many women, I invite you to ask yourself or the women you know how they feel about their age, beauty and/or body. If they experience negative feelings about these, it's clear that they (likely unconsciously) buy into the outdated notion that attaches a woman's worth to her body.

Health Tip:
These body and/or image altering techniques alone or in combination with the underlying psychology that has led to their employment can seriously impact women's health[8].

Health Implications:
Stress
Anxiety
Depression
Body dysmorphia
Disturbed body image
Feelings of powerlessness
Unhealthy eating and/or
exercising behaviors
Lowered confidence, self esteem
and/or self worth
and so much more ...

Other Ways This Issue Can Manifest:
Social isolation
Spiritual distress
Abusive relationships
Inability to thrive
Negative and/or abusive self talk
Inability to cope with new life
situations
and so much more

However, by recognizing that we, as a collective culture, still (clearly unconsciously) uphold outdated philosophies and social scripts, we give a voice to the silent battle women experience.

In breaking the silence, the space for social transformation is created.

In fact, it is clear that we are sitting on the cusp of a *powerful* revolution!

Evidence of this revolution can be seen in small movements around the world ...

However, before these socially innovative movements are exposed, let's pause to frame the revolution by exploring both the past and the present of the construct of "sexy."

History proves that sexual desirability related to physical beauty changes with time and place.

Clear examples of this include: plump women are considered the most desirable in some countries[9], whereas women with the most stretch in their neck (via strategically placed gold rings) are considered the most beautiful in others[10].

Even within North American culture, it wasn't until Twiggy came along in the 1960s that ultra thin became the perception for what was considered sexually appealing[11]. Before then, curvy women like Marilyn Monroe were considered feminine and desirable[12].

These examples indicate that beauty and/or sexy are not only culturally determined, but also vary according to the historical time period.

---

9 In some African countries, women enter "fattening periods" to boost their beauty.
10 In Burma, female members of the Kayan tribe wear rings on their neck as a sign of beauty.
11 This perception does not necessarily reflect the true wants of a woman's romantic partner. However, it may be what creates much of the body/beauty anxiety and stress women experience.

In other words, beauty and sexy are not fixed concepts.

Instead, they are socially constructed and ever evolving.

However, it seems that we, as a culture, have forgotten that *it is possible* to change the assumption of how sexy is "supposed to be expressed" so that it truly matches contemporary views.

Below are several examples of how this outdated vision of sexy currently impacts the quality of life of women and girls in this culture:

1. Girls as young as five years old verbalizing that they feel the need to diet, not because they are fat but because they are aware, even at their tender age, of monstrous expectations related to their physical beauty and body shape[13].

2. Beauty is a global 160 billion dollar a year industry[14]. The vast majority of spending is done by women. This points to the reality that women feel the need to "become" beautiful, rather than surrendering into the REALity that they already are .

3. Women silently battling with themselves by engaging negative self talk and/or non-health-based behaviors (i.e. certain diets and/ or exercise regimes) - in an effort to physically portray the status quo for feminine beauty (i.e. young, fit and beautiful)[15].

4. Women feeling the need to compete with each other (silently and/or vocally) over beauty, body size, breast size, etc., making genuine, nurturing friendships with other women seem impossible[16].

5. Many women aren't able to accept the honest compliments that come their way.[17] The rampant nature of this phenomenon

---

15 Instead of academic research, ask yourself the honest question of how you engage in negative self talk or non love-based behaviors that make you feel less than miraculous, incredibly delicious you.
16 This point is the #1 ranking issue women vocalize within Sexy ... it's not that serious™ workshops.
17 Again, ask yourself and/or the women you know about this. Do they consistently receive the compliments they are given? Or, do they brush them off and/or minimize their deservedness? If they do the latter, what is the cause?

indicates that this occurs not due to modesty but rather due to many women not being able to see their own incredible value and worth.

Food For Thought:
If a person is truly happy would they really feel the need to embody another person's vision of "perfection"? Or, would they be happy enough to be themselves? Sexy (beauty/the body/age) is not that serious. Happiness is ...

Thankfully, thought leaders from around the globe have noticed how profoundly women's lives can be impacted when they feel expected to fit inside ill fitting **boxes**.

In turn, various opportunities have been created for women and/or girls to examine and/or redefine what they have been taught about sexy, beauty and their body so they can choose to step forward into new, empowering ways of being.

These opportunities are individual movements within the global revolution.

Examples of these movements include:

1. Women becoming restless and gently demanding – with their spending dollars – images that reflect authentic beauty; real humans. In turn, some corporations are listening and responding accordingly. Examples of progressive campaigns include: Dove's Campaign for Real Beauty where women of all shapes, sizes, ethnicities, and ages are used to showcase what real women, bodies and beauty can look like[18].

2. Images and messages that validate the power and perfection of authentic feminine expression. For example: celebrities choosing

to be showcased on the cover of magazines without makeup and/
or refusing to have their photos retouched by PhotoShop. These
actions demonstrate – to the masses – that a woman's worth is not
solely grounded in her physicality. In fact, women can still be granted power, visibility, social worth *and* be considered desirable and
sexy in her authentic, unaltered and natural state.

3. Countless communities, blogs, Twitter feeds and Facebook pages
dedicated to female empowerment and/or sisterhood. Some examples include:

- Real Women Have Curves[19]: A FaceBook page dedicated to
  celebrating confident, classy and sexy women who embrace
  their bodies.

- Beauty Redefined: A web page dedicated to "helping wom-
  en and girls recognize and reject harmful messages about
  their bodies and what "beauty" means and looks like."[20]
  The author loves this site for 2 reasons: 1) because it is an
  accessible resource for people so they can empower themselves to make decisions about their body, beauty and sexy
  and 2) because it's been created by two doctoral (PhD)
  candidates and is grounded in research.

- The New Wave[21] founded by Marsh Engle of Los Angeles,
  California. This movement is dedicated to redefining the
  culture of a woman's success and has been designed to help
  women embody their authentic power in order to innovate
  change, not only in their own lives but also in the lives of
  others. The author loves this organization because it is also
  gives back to the community by offering single mothers
  opportunities for a better life.

- Fit Chicks[22] is a Canada wide, women's only fitness
  company dedicated to providing fun, fierce and supportive
  programs for women to reach their full potential - inside

and out. The author loves this organization because the people within this business really walk their talk. Having been a fitness professional for over 15 years, the author knows it's rare to find fitness organizations that are transparent, client centered and filled with love. It's delicious that this one is.

- The Heart of Flourishing[23] is a physical and online community dedicated to helping men and women live flourishing lives. The founder, Tara Antler, is a master at helping people fall in love with themselves and step into flourishing lives.

- Sexy Sisterhood: A movement birthed in Los Angeles, CA by the author. The premise for this movement is to support women of all ages, shapes and backgrounds shift their consciousness and heal their relationships with their bodies so they can step into exquisitely delicious lives.

4. Cover Girl Culture[24]: A film directed by Nicole Clark about the impact media has on our society. Clark now speaks in grade schools and high schools, educating young women and girls about the ways media can impact their views about their body, beauty, worth and esteem. The author believes Nicole's message is very powerful because it meets girls at the community level and educates them so they can become empowered, which is a step towards protecting their mental health.

5. Misty Tripoli[26]: A warrior for truth and Founder of The World Groove Movement. Misty travels the world teaching her revolutionary Groove Method, helping free people from their fears so they can taste the bliss of moving their bodies and dancing authentically.

6. Sensual movement and pole classes, lap dance lessons and other means for women to step into their sexy through dance and movement. You can find local classes in dance and fitness centers near you. (Please note: The author recognizes that many sensuality based

fitness and dance classes are still based on the old paradigms of "sexy/beauty/the body" and "getting it right." To protect yourself from **sensual whiplash** and experience what *authentic* sensual movement feels like, please explore Spin Buddies[25] sensual movement classes or Misty Tripoli's Risqué Groove class[26]).

7. The series 50 Shades of Gray[27] depicts a woman who is hungry to explore and express her authentic sexuality. The global popularity of these books, as indicated by large numbers of women devouring them, demonstrates how intriguing it is for women to learn that authentic sexual expression is possible for them. This knowledge is the key to them becoming empowered (how delicious!).

8. Oprah Winfrey[28] providing opportunities for real women to take part in a fashion shoot for O magazine. *All* women want to feel beautiful, sexy and visible. It's so delicious that Oprah makes it possible for them!

The movements indicated here are only a handful of what is occurring around the globe regarding women stepping into new expressions of themselves. However, these various examples provide clear indications that a global revolution is brewing because they highlight a common thread - an unspoken Truth: women are tired of not feeling good enough and are ready to step into a safe space that allows them to be fully expressed.

They want to feel beautiful, successful, vibrant, happy and sexy - on their own terms.

In fact, they *deserve* to be acknowledged for all the goodness that they are - regardless of their age, weight, beauty, pant size, etc. ..

Okay Gorgeous!

What are your thoughts?

Are you ready to join the revolution?

Powerful Truth:

When sexy is redefined, a woman cannot get sexy wrong simply because she is both defining it for herself and molding it to a framework that she already knows and understands – her life.
In turn, she is able to dramatically boost her quality of life and step into NEW levels of confidence, power and esteem.

NOTES

1 Steele, T., (2005). *Sex, self and society: The social context of sexuality* (1st ed.). Kentucky: Cenage.

2 Haas, C. F., Champion, A. & Secor, D. (2008). Motivating factors for seeking cosmetic surgery: A synthesis of the literature. *Plastic Surgical Nursing, 28(4)*, p 177-182. Retrieved from ProQuest Nursing

Hurd Clarke, L & Griffin, M. (2008). Visible and invisible ageing: Beauty work as a response to ageism. *Aging & Society, 28*, 653-674. Retrieved from ProQuest Nursing

Hurd Clarke, L. & Griffin, M. (2007). Becoming and being gendered through the body: Older women, their mothers and body image. *Ageing and Society, 27*, p. 701-719. Retrieved from ProQuest Nursing

3 Bedford, J. L. & Johnson, C. S. (2006). Societal influences on body image dissatisfaction in younger and older women. *Journal of Women and Aging, 18(1)*, p 41-55. Retrieved from ProQuest Nursing

Crerand, C. E., Infield, A. L. & Sarwer, D. B. (2007). Pyschological considerations in cosmetic breast augmentation. *Plastic Surgical Nursing, 27(3)*, p 146-152. Retrieved from Pro Quest Nursing

Hurd Clarke, L & Griffin, M. (2008). Visible and invisible ageing: Beauty work as a response to ageism. *Aging & Society, 28*, 653-674. Retrieved from ProQuest Nursing

Rudd, N. & Lennon, S. (2000). Body image and appearance-management behaviors in college women. *Cothing and Textiles Research Journal, 18(3)*, p 152-162. Retrieved from Sage Journals

4 Comment found within a footnote in the text.

5 Bedford, J. L. & Johnson, C. S. (2006). Societal influences on body image dissatisfaction in younger and older women. *Journal of Women and Aging, 18(1)*, p 41-55. Retrieved from ProQuest Nursing

McCormick, M. L. (2008). Women's bodies aging: Culture, context, and social work practice. *Journal of Women and Social Work, 23(4)*, p 312-323. Retrieved from ProQuest Nursing

6 Haas, C. F., Champion, A. & Secor, D. (2008). Motivating factors for seeking cosmetic surgery: A synthesis of the literature. *Plastic Surgical Nursing, 28(4)*, 177-182. Retrieved from ProQuest Nursing

Hurd Clarke, L & Griffin, M. (2008). Visible and invisible ageing: Beauty work as a response to ageism. *Aging & Society, 28*, 653-674. Retrieved from ProQuest Nursing

7 Bedford, J. L. & Johnson, C. S. (2006). Societal influences on body image dissatisfaction in younger and older women. *Journal of Women and Aging, 18(1)*, 41-55. Retrieved from ProQuest Nursing

Farchaus Stein, K & Corte, C. (2008). The identity impairment model: A longitudinal study of self-schemas as predictors of disordered eating behaviors. *Nursing Research, 57(3)*, 182–190

8 Brown, A. & Dittmar, H. (2005). Think "thin" and feel bad: The role of appearance schema activation, attention level, and thin-ideal internalization for young women's responses to ultra thin media ideals. *Journal of Social and Clinical Psychology, 24(8),* 1088-1113

Crerand, C. E., Infield, A. L. & Sarwer, D. B. (2007). Pyschological considerations in cosmetic breast augmentation. *Plastic Surgical Nursing, 27(3),* p 146-152. Retrieved from Pro-Quest Nursing

Haas, C. F., Champion, A. & Secor, D. (2008). Motivating factors for seeking cosmetic surgery: A synthesis of the literature. *Plastic Surgical Nursing, 28(4),* p 177-182. Retrieved from ProQuest Nursing

Hurd Clarke, L. & Griffin, M. (2007). Becoming and being gendered through the body: Older women, their mothers and body image. *Ageing and Society, 27,* 701-719. Retrieved from ProQuest Nursing

Hurd Clarke, L & Griffin, M. (2008). Visible and invisible ageing: Beauty work as a response to ageism. *Aging & Society, 28,* 653-674. Retrieved from ProQuest Nursing

McCormick, M. L. (2008). Women's bodies aging: Culture, context, and social work practice. *Journal of Women and Social Work, 23(4),* 312-323. Retrieved from ProQuest Nursing

Mills, J., Polivy, J., Herman, C.P. & Tiggerman, M. (2002). Effects of exposure to thin media images: Evidence of self-enhancement among restrained eaters. Retrieved from http://web4.uwindsor.ca/users/j/jarry/main.nsf/032ecd0df8f83bdf8525699900571a93/aa9ed943e56182bf85256abe005bc3f6/$FILE/Mills%20et%20al%20(2002).pdf

Pollay, R.W. (1986). The distorted mirror: Reflections on the unintended consequences of advertising. *Journal of Marketing. 50(April)*, p 18-36

Richins, M.L. (1991). Social comparison and the idealized images of advertising. *Journal of Consumer Research, 18 (June)*, p 71-83

Stice, E., & Shaw, H. (1994). Adverse effects of the media portrayed thin-ideal on women, and linkages to bulimic symptomatology. *Journal of Social and Clinical Psychology, 13*, p 288-308

9 Women's Revolution (n.d.). Fattening rooms in Africa stir different perceptions of beauty. Retrieved from http://www.womensrevolution.com/2011/05/fattening-rooms-in-africa-stir. html

10 Anitei, S. (2006, October). The 'Giraffe' Women of the Neck Rings. Softpedia. Retrieved from http://news.softpedia.com/news/The-Giraffe-Women-of-the-Neck-Rings-37412.shtml

11 Comment found within a footnote in the text.

12 Wikipedia/ "Female Body Shapes," 2012. http://en.wikipedia.org/wiki/Female_body_shape

13 Smyth, G. (n.d.) Women's Body Image in Canada and The Facts. *Self.ca*. Retrieved from http://www.self.ca/articles/health_and_wellness/emotional_well_being/canadian_womens_body_image/

Abramovitz B. & Birch L.(2000). Five-Year-Old Girls' Ideas About Dieting are Predicted by Their Mothers' Dieting. *Journal of the American Dietetic Association, 20(3),* 1157-1163. Retrieved from http://www.ncbi.nlm.nih.gov/pmc/articles/PMC2530935/

14 The Economist. (2003, May 22). Pots of promise. Retrieved from http://www.economist.com/node/1795852

15 Comment found within a footnote in the text.

16 Comment found within a footnote in the text.

17 Comment found within a footnote in the text.

18 Unilever (2012). The Dove campaign for real beauty. http://www.dove.us/Social-Mission/campaign-for-real-beauty.aspx

19 Real Women Have Curves
http://www.facebook.com/RealWomenHaveCurvesFan

20 Beauty Redefined (n.d.) Beauty redefined: About us.
http://www.beautyredefined.net/about-us

21 The New Wave
http://www.thewomansmovement.com

22 Fit Chicks
http://www.fitchicks.ca

23 The Heart of Flourishing
http://www.theheartofflourishing.com

24 Cover Girl Culture
http://www.covergirlculture.com

25 Spin Buddies Pole Studio
http://www.spinbuddies.com

26 Misty Tripoli
http://www.mistytripoli.com &
http://www.TheWorldGrooveMovement.com

27 James, E.L., 2011. *Fifty shades of grey*. New York: Vintage.

28 Oprah.com (2012). Be a model in O's Real Women fashion
shoots! Retrieved from https://www.oprah.com/ownshow/
plug_form.html?plug_id=714&cc=CA

CHAPTER TWO
Wake up, Beautiful!
It is safe to be authentically sexy

---

*Embodying Authentic Sexy Opens
You To NEW Levels of Confidence
And Personal Power*

I t is safe to be authentically sexy.

Let's pause with that thought for a moment and breathe life into its REALity.

That's right.

Even though *we know* that what we've been taught about sexy, our bodies, our worth and our value is not true, *we have yet to be taught* how to validate our inner lady while feeling safe enough to shine our authentic sexy for the world to see.

Thankfully, as of right now, this Truth is no longer valid.

As I have already mentioned, this book experience is meant to help you bridge:

1) *what you know* (that your age, beauty, body and/or how you express sexy are NOT what truly gives you worth) with
2) *feeling safe enough* to embody your unique expression of sexy in ways that honor you.

As your tour guide, it is my duty to shine the light on where your authentic sexy lives.

I am also here to remind you that sexy isn't something to run from.

In fact, it's ridiculously delicious.

The fact is that as women we need to learn how to embrace our sexy – on our own terms and in ways that feel great to us.

This means that we need to learn how to **own** our authentic sexy powerfully so we can shine even brighter, feel even freer, and love even deeper.

In fact, the confidence boost you will experience as a result of owning your authentic sexy just might draw your perfect mate to you or help you heal and/or grow a relationship you are already in!

It also might help you heal your relationship with money and professional success because you will understand that it is safe for you to shine and ask for your worth.

It also might help you expand relationships with other women because authentic sexy gives space for all women to be exceptional.

Because when you embrace authentic sexy, the need for comparison and competition dies.

It also might help you heal the relationship you have with your body because you will finally feel *good enough*, as you are right now.

Gorgeous, I have to be honest and tell you something: I have this incredible ability to see through paper and I want you to know that I can see the **real you.**

Even though the most important person on the planet may not be able to.

Yes, I'm referring to you. YOU are the most important person in the world, my beauty.

And because I can see the real you, I am just going to say it ...

You are stunning and amazing.

In fact, WOW!

You, my beautiful Sexy Sister, are the most beautiful creature on planet earth.

I think it's time for you to own this Truth.

Yes, in case you are wondering, it *IS* possible for each and every woman to be the most beautiful creature on the planet.

How?

It's simple.

Each one of us has our own unique expression of beauty ... our unique and perfect version of sexy.

Therefore, we are unrepeatable.

This makes the absence of comparison and competition possible.

Can you see how internalizing this Truth makes it possible for you to stop judging yourself against other beautiful women and OWN your beauty for yourself?

Besides, there is more than enough beauty and authentic sexy to go around!

Additionally, when sexy and beauty are redefined to fit your age, curves, personality and life, they become incredibly easy to get right!

After all, the only thing you have to do be you.

Beautiful, delicious, incredibly SEXY you.

It's okay if you have never before been able to see or believe how beautiful and amazing you are.

However, I can assure you that it *is* the Truth.

I can also tell you that it may take some time for you to really accept this Truth, depending on how much **programming** you have to **UNlearn**.

Chances are you are like most women. You spend time focusing on what you don't like about yourself – your perceived imperfections – rather than focusing on your positives features.

Notice I say "perceived imperfections."

Your perceived imperfections are what YOU don't like about you. Did you ever think that other people actually delight in your "imperfections"? That your imperfections endear you to others?

You've learned to dismiss aspects of your beauty, beingness, power and worth and, in turn, live aspects of your life in ways that do not *truly* honor all of the goodness that you are ...

And it is no longer working for you!

You are ready for change.

You are ready to experience life on your terms - as a confident, powerful and authentically sexy woman.

How do you think your life would be if you finally became friends with your body?

If you started to feel comfortable in your own skin and own the fact that you are absolutely perfect and sexy *even with* all your **perfect imperfections?**

What if you learned how to focus on and celebrate your attributes rather than your flaws?

Or if you learned that it is OKAY (better than okay even!) to love and explore your sexy side?

How would life be different if you felt completely safe to be authentically sexy?

Sweetheart, I have a secret ...

It *is* safe.

It is also safe for you to live in harmony with your age/body/beauty/ sexy rather than resist them.

Albert Einstein hit the nail on the head by defining insanity as, "… doing the same thing over and over again and expecting different results."

What are you doing or thinking over and over again that is not permitting you to live a vibrantly happy and flourishing life?

Do you really think it will change if you don't take action?

If you're wondering how you take action ... it's easy.

All you have to do is choose.

Choose to wake up.

Choose to let go of ways of being that aren't serving you in order to grow into an even brighter, more radiant expression of authentic sensual you.

The beautiful, incredible, miraculous, lovable you.

The (**you**)**nique** and irreplaceable you.

The you you were born to be.

By waking up you can say, "So what if the media and our culture focus almost exclusively on the female body as the barometer for feminine worth and value? I am free to choose to adopt those beliefs ... or not."

Waking up is understanding that you have the choice to be hyper-self-conscious about your body ... or to love your body, as it is, because it's the only one you've got.

Waking up means giving yourself permission to love yourself, as you are – regardless of your age, gender, religion, class, race, education, appearance, marital status, sense of style, etc., etc., etc.

Waking up is being courageous to simply be – *even when* everyone around you has an opinion or thought about how you *should* be.

Waking up means you have the confidence to live your Truth.

Your sexy, delicious, feminine, yummy Truth.

So?

How about it, Beautiful?

Are you ready to take action and wake up?

Are you ready to step into a definition of sexy that amplifies
all of the goodness that you are?

I sure hope so ...

Because your authentic sexy is waiting.

For an exercise to help you identify your authentic
beauty - a key element in your expression of deliciousness- please
turn to pages 151 & 152.

Powerful Truth:
Women not feeling safe enough to be
sexy - on their own terms and in their
own ways - is a First World Human
Rights Issue.

CHAPTER THREE
From body shame to finding authentic sexy

*The Key To Authentic Sexy
Is Letting Go Of What You Thought It
Was And Having The Courage To
Define It For Yourself*

I have to be totally honest, because I like to keep it real …

I have *known* for many years that my body isn't supposed to define me. However, I have *felt* like I was not "good enough," as in sexy enough, pretty enough, fit enough in some way, shape or form pretty much my entire life.

In other words, even though I knew the Truth, I hadn't the foggiest idea of how to embody it!

In fact, it was evident that "not feeling good enough" was my underlying programming or way of engaging with the world.

This underlying programming revealed itself to me in many ways such as:

engaging negative self-talk;

working out too much for aesthetic reasons versus for health

Editor's Note:
Interesting how you "have known" but you "have felt." There is a clear dichotomy between mind and body or thoughts and feelings.

reasons;

and not eating enough in order to control my body size (I am not talking about anorexia nervosa, rather **disordered eating**).

I'd judge myself for pretty much everything;

punish myself by continuing the negative self talk;

and compound it with being unkind to myself and not giving myself space or time to just be.

Another common way my self-worth issues were evident was when I would look at myself in the mirror and absolutely *hate* everything I saw.

Retrospectively, I can see how sad it was that for so many years I was completely blind to my positive features.

Sure, I was able to function.

Have a job.

Go to school.

But in many of my private moments I was my own worst enemy.

In fact, I secretly waged World War III on my body every day!

I unconsciously bought into the idea that, as a woman in this society, my body should DEFINE me *even though* (I thought) I knew better.

The truth was that deep down some part of me believed that if I didn't have a perfect body or look like a model or famous actress then I could never *truly* be happy.

In other words, I felt I had to earn happy by fitting into an image that was unachievable for me simply due to the REALity that my genetic makeup makes it impossible for me to fit into our culture's constructed vision of feminine physical perfection.

My genetics gifted me with lovely breasts, a fleshy buttocks and a medium built frame.

I can't deny that.

However, for a long time I also couldn't accept that, which was a definite source of much emotional pain.

Health Tip:
Size double zero is not physiologically possible for most women.

Moreover, I couldn't understand why I was so hung up on my body. *Especially because* I had so many wonderful qualities and features in my life - over and above my physical attributes - that gave me value and worth such as: earning a university degree, being a skilled educator, being able to do the work I love, as well as being able to forge and maintain rewarding friendships with amazing people.

Essentially, I had every reason to be happy.

So why did I let "sexy" hold such power over me?

Deep down I knew I wasn't taking "crazy pills" because a singular definition of sexy didn't fit me, my personality or my curves.

I also knew that *even though* social messaging was subtly trying to make me believe that I wasn't good enough, I knew I was.

It was at that moment that I realized that I had to take a stand and find the Truth.

It became time for me to redefine sexy and desirability so I could feel valuable - on every level - not just within work, family, friends, sports and academia.

I was ready to feel good in my own skin and be sexy - on my own terms - for no other reason that because it would please ME!

Thus began my voyage; my right of passage to transform an ill fitting concept of sexy into *my* unique reflection of sexy: an authentic expression of my joyful spirit and beautiful heart.

It was on this passage that I learned how to see beyond the smoke-and-mirrors of social messaging – what's being said and what's not being said.

It was also on this path that I came face to face with a Gorgeous Goddess named Truth.

She lovingly smacked me in the face and woke me to the REALity that I had been lying to myself.

Lying so that I could continue to believe that I wasn't good enough and, in turn, continue to play small with my life.

Lying by spinning stories to keep myself stuck in a pattern of embodying outdated, dis-empowering messages.

Lying to myself by *believing* what I was told was the Truth versus what I *knew* was true and right for me – especially when my views, ideas and beliefs were different than what I had been taught.

In fact, I had no idea (until I really thought about it) how influential our cultural frames and expectations are for women - regarding being sexy, desirable and beautiful.

For example, we are subtly taught that a woman is supposed to be either:

smart OR sexy,

kind OR desirable,

beautiful OR mature.

However, I knew I embodied all facets.

In fact, I know I am:

sexy AND smart,

kind AND desirable,

beautiful AND older than most of the mainstream depictions of sexy.

In fact, right down to my DNA, I *knew* that these authentic ways I expressed life contributed to the uniqueness of me! Because of that Truth, how could I be expected to be someone other than who I authentically am?

(More importantly, why was I listening?!?)

I was tired of trying to fit into society's view of what my sexy expression should look like.

Monitoring my behavior was exhausting.

It did not feel good to hide.

What's more is that as time passed, it dawned on me that I had no guarantee of tomorrow.

The thought of letting my life pass by me without fully embracing and enjoying both my authentic sexy and all the gifts it brings gave me the courage to stop hiding and start BEING me immediately, everyday!

With that, I made the choice to take responsibility for my happiness and discover new ways to both think and live my life.

Using nothing but the quiet and truthful whisperings of my intuition and heart, I "emptied my backpack" (meaning I left behind the previous ways I had looked at the world, my life and my body).

In doing so, I had to take responsibility for everything I put in my backpack; both what was serving me and what I had outgrown.

If I chose to carry heavy, ill fitting ideas about my life, body and/or way I expressed sexy, it was my choice and I had to assume the load.

Believe me, when you have to carry everything consciously, it makes letting go of the unnecessary views and beliefs easy!

How well my backpack fit me taught me how to find the path of least resistance.

If it was heavy, I was carrying something that didn't belong to me because I knew my *authentic expression* was light.

My authenticity isn't a burden because it is chalk full of YUM; a living **animation** of the truth of who I am, which is energizing, uplifting and feels soooooo delicious!

Because I found the courage to engage my Truth, I found a profoundly liberating nugget to put in my backpack.

The Truth I found is this: I can really, truly TRUST myself.

In fact, I was able to see that the decisions I make *always* lead me towards my best and juiciest life; as long as I remember trust my heart's whisperings and **en-JOY** the process of the journey.

With this new way of being, I was able to allow the delightful flow of my life carry me to new experiences that I never before knew were possible!

In fact, I was finally carried to what I had been searching for ... the key to my expression of authentic sexy.

Authentic sexy is accessible to me in every minute of every day because it's interwoven with my DNA. However, the only key that has the power to unlock this gift is having the courage to love myself, as I am.

Ultimately, I discovered that I had unknowingly been holding myself captive inside *my own* feelings of "not good enough!"

Not realizing *that it was possible* for me to take responsibility, left me unconsciously giving my power away instead of stepping into my authentic sexy.

"Not good enough" was a cage I put myself in and, in turn, the lens from which I viewed my life.

How I Learned This Truth:

I was working on the set of Discovery Channel's "Sex Files" and "Sexual Secrets" portraying various archetypes of female sexuality.

I remember feeling hideously fat and TOTALLY self-conscious! However, I decided to squash those feelings of self doubt and insecurity so I could remain present and do my best for the camera.

The shoot ended and a few months later the shows could be viewed on various television stations.

For some reason I didn't get to see myself on the small screen for years. However, many of my friends did and told me I looked great and did an awesome job.

Little did they know that while they were complimenting me, in my head and heart I was cringing thinking that they were lying, trying to protect my feelings.

All I could think about was how I felt during filming. (I felt that I looked more like an Orca whale than like the sexy, gorgeous woman I was being paid to portray).

I believed my perception of reality must be everyone's view and therefore remained stuck in my personal judgments – unable to see the possibility that the compliments may actually have been deserved.

Several years later, when I finally saw myself on TV for the first time, I was shocked that I *didn't* look hideous and fat.

In fact, objectively speaking, I actually looked really good!

I was stunned that the way I *actually* looked was a far cry from the way I *thought* looked.

It was then and there that I realized that sexy is not *that* serious.

... Okay, okay, you got me. It *was* super serious when I was in my head!

The truth is that I was so hard on myself because *in my head* I didn't think I look like my vision of what a model should look like.

However, looking back, if I knew then what I know now - that "just being me" and doing my best is always perfect – I would have saved myself a lot of emotional grief!

The gift of learning that sexy is not *that* serious also taught me that when I shine my authentic light to the world - *even if* I have self doubt or am not feeling 100% confident - I am okay. Better than okay even. Perfect! … If there is such a thing.

Powerful Point:
It's important to get out of your head if you want to experience the power and deliciousness that lives inside your authentic sexy.

Why?

Because it became crystal clear that my view of reality and REALity are not always synonymous. Especially regarding my body and/or being sexy.

In fact, I learned that I had to STOP trying to "DO" sexy (because that meant I was in my head).

Instead, I had to learn how to BE sexy - on my own terms and in my own ways so that I felt honored, nourished and incredibly delicious.

The Grand Irony Is This:
You can't BE authentically sexy if you are trying to DO sexy!

Why?

Because authentic sexy isn't complicated.

In fact, it's very simple and comes from inside of you, which is why it's not something you can "put on" - like makeup or a dress.

It's also why it's not something that only a select few can "get right."

The fact is this: authentic sexy is accessible to everyone.

If you want to experience the Truth of this statement, all you have to do is take responsibility for feeling "good enough."

Sexy Truth:
Authentic sexy is not complicated.
It's also not for the elite.
In fact, it's as simple and accessible as breathing.

Alright, Beautiful?

Are you ready to become friends with your body?

To redefine sexy to fit YOUR curves, age, personality and life?

To find your (you)nique expression of authentic sexy,
as defined by you?

After all, you *already are* incredibly sexy - you just have to learn how to authentically BE it!

For exercises to help you awaken and explore your unique expression of authentic sexy, please turn to pages 123-127.

CHAPTER FOUR
FUNdamental truths about sexy

---

*Sexy Is Not That Serious. In Fact,
Redefining It To Fit Your Age, Curves,
Personality And Life Makes
Embodying Sexy A Lot Of FUN
(Not To Mention Nourishing)!*

Who made up the rule that sexy
has to be serious? I believe that if you
didn't make it up, you don't have to
subscribe to it!

(And even if you DID make it up, you
can always change your mind and
choose to see sexy as fun, playful
and empowering!).

FUNdamental Truth One:
You are not "broken."

You Are Exquisitely Delicious
As You Are.

W ould you believe me if I told you that you are not broken?

In fact, did you know that you are exquisitely delicious as you are?

Even with your cellulite and wrinkles.

Even with your hormonal cycles and chaotic life.

However, I'd be willing to bet that someone, somewhere planted a seed in your mind that told you that something is wrong with you.

That seed took root and grew into self doubt or other forms of insecurity.

Those insecurities have manifested in your life in many ways, such as through dieting, purchasing anti-aging lotions, negative self talk, frustration with your body, and feeling like you are never quite "good enough" to name a few common examples.

However, I can assure you that you are *not broken*. In fact, you are PERFECT, as you are!

I recognize that you probably think I am crazy for even saying that.

(Honestly, that response breaks my heart a little and makes me wish I could scoop you into an ENORMOUS hug and squeeze all those "broken-self" thoughts right out of you! That being said, I understand that this may be the first time you ever have heard this Truth, so it might seem a little strange).

The Truth is that you are a MIRACLE.

Why?

Because there is no one else on this planet who is exactly like you.

In fact, you are (you)nique and the only person who is 100% perfect at being you!

It's unfortunate that as members of this particular social group we are taught to keep striving to fit inside an unamed box that may not reflect our true needs for experiencing an optimal quality of life.

For example, we are told to:

DO more!

FIX this!

GET more!

HEAL that!

BE this!

DON'T be that!

We are bombarded EVERYDAY with both explicit and implicit messages about:

HOW to be.

WHAT to wear.

HOW to act.

How NOT to act.

HOW to feel.

How NOT to feel.

… and the list goes on.

As a result, feeling that we ARE broken - related to the concept of sexy (i.e. our age/beauty/body/weight/etc.) - has become very real indeed.

In fact, I am sure you have experienced these "broken self pains" at some point in your life ...

They may have manifested as low feelings of self worth or confidence related to your age, body, size, shape, weight, beauty and/or background.

They may have expressed through your feelings and/or perceptions like: anxiety, stress or depression; disordered and unhealthy eating or exercising patterns, or even through body dysmorphic disorder - where you can't perceive you **beautiful body** as it is.

They may even look like a complete (or partial) disconnection from your authentic expression of sexy. This means that you do not define for yourself what sexy looks like or feels like for you.

The unfortunate Truth is that these pains are so common that most of us believe that they are "normal!"

In fact, the messages that communicate that we are broken anchor us into a harmful cycle that powerfully impacts both our health and quality of life.

And because these broken self messages occur so frequently, most of us never realize that there is another way!

However, what if I told you that everything you do and everything you are is just fine?

It's true.

You are not broken.

Period.

To frame the possibility of this REALity I have two questions to ask you, Beautiful:

1) Are the "lenses" you have been wearing through which you perceive that you are broken and need to fix yourself making you feel good about yourself?

If not,

2) Do you know it actually IS possible for you to feel sexy on your own terms and delicious in every moment of every day?

The simple Truth is this: YOU do not have to change. Because you are perfect, as you are.

Instead, it's our culture's view and pressures regarding the concept of SEXY that has to change.

I imagine you are starting to gather by now that sexy really isn't what you thought it was ...

Okay, Gorgeous. If this concept of truly feeling good about yourself is new to you (or if you want to experience the Truth of it even more), I invite you to come and play with me.

Take the concept of being whole for a test drive.

See how it feels.

See how it responds to your curves ...

For an exercise designed to highlight all your "unbroken" features and qualities, please turn to page 149 & 150.

You are the only person on this
planet who is 100% perfect
at being you!

FUNdamental Truth Two
You are (YOU)nique!

"Why fit in when you were born to stand out?"
Dr. Seuss

N o one can "do" you like YOU do you.

So, (obviously) it's important for you to BE you…in all your amazing glory.

This includes being your:

DELICIOUS THOUGHTFUL INSPIRING

GOOFY CUTE WEIRD

PLAYFUL OVER-THE-TOP KIND

FUNNY QUIRKY CALM

FABULOUS FIERCE FEISTY SEXY

PATIENT SNAZZY RELAXED

PENSIVE JOYFUL VIBRANT

BOUNCY SMART SASSY

QUIET ROCK STAR (fill in the blank) SELF!

Essentially, I am giving you permission to experience life in the ways that feel best to you – for no other reason than because they make you happy.

I am sure you already know many of these sides of yourself but reserve them for certain people and/or certain circumstances (such as when you are at work or at home).

You're probably used to playing a role and/or putting on a **mask** in different contexts and are not accustomed to thinking that it IS possible for you to express all aspects of your beautiful and amazing personality anytime you please.

This former way of being is totally OK. However, as of today your masks are going to be put in storage – only to be used on Halloween (or possibly during kinky nights with your sweetie *wink).

In other words, as of right now, your **on reserve attitude** is going to change.

Today you are going to *give yourself permission* to let loose and just BE (regardless of where you are and who is around).

After all, you are (you)nique, therefore welcomed (and encouraged!) to let your **FREAK FLAG** fly high!

For a fun exercise designed to help you explore your (you)nique Freak Flag expression, please go to page 173.

FUNdamental Truth Three
Your body is a meat suit.
It cannot define you.
YOU define you.

Allowing Your Body To Be What It Is
- A Meat Suit – And Choosing To Define
YOU Based On YOU Is Authentically Sexy.

Your body is a meat suit; a bag of bones, muscles, organs and skin.

The Truth about your body not defining you is specifically related to your worth not being anchored to the look/age/shape/size/beauty of your body.

Because the fact is this: you are WAY more than "just" your body.

Your body is only one aspect that comprises your being.

However, you do live in a body, so taking care of it is important. Not only because it allows you to exist, but also because it provides a physical structure from which to animate yourself and your life.

Taking care of yourself means respecting your body - your meat suit - by eating healthy foods to nourish yourself so that you have energy to live your life and accomplish your goals and dreams.

This also means drinking plenty of water.

Engaging in nurturing self care activities that make you feel valuable and delicious (see page 170 for an exercise to uncover your (e)sensual self care preferences).

Making time for powerful stress management techniques like taking walks and doing yoga, breath work and meditation.

It also means moving your body (via exercise) because the human body is designed to move.

It is important to do things that make you feel good about yourself.

Having a high sense of self esteem and worth is vital for experiencing a vibrantly happy life.

Truth:
In this day and age most people don't get as much exercise as their beautiful bodies need.

Additionally, because a woman's body no longer defines her, she can *choose* to experience the pressure of embodying stereotypical beauty ideals – or not.

Let's pause with that thought for a moment.

Women now have the right to choose to fit into socially constructed ideas about feminine beauty OR they can choose to ACCEPT the size they are and RESPECT their meat suit (and protect their mental, emotional and physical health!).

By choosing to accept their body and respect it – at whatever size it is – women are taking the first steps to embodying the REALity that their body (age, beauty and curves) *truly* do not define them or dictate how valuable, visible or desirable they are. In other words, by loving their body as it is, they take back their power.

Additionally, part of respecting your body is taking on the responsibility to care for yourself in ways that honor your *own* health boundaries.

If you are too small or too big than what your body needs in order to function at an optimal level then you may experience health problems.

Therefore, it's true that your body - your meat suit - does not define you.

However, it can demonstrate how you *really feel* about yourself.

Why?

Because as humans, we have the capacity to choose how we behave.

Therefore, our actions can demonstrate how we *truly* feel about ourselves.

Do we eat enough?

Or too much?

Do we exercise enough?

Or too much?

Do we rest as much as we need?

Play as much as we can?

Or, do we lack balance?

Do we practice loving and nurturing self-care?

Truth:
Feeling good about yourself is not something someone is able to do for you. It comes from the inside. It's a gift you give to yourself.

Or, do we abuse ourselves in some way, shape or form?

Our actions tell us how valuable we see ourselves and our lives.

How happy and full of life we feel we deserve to be.

How lovable and worthy we feel we are.

Okay, Gorgeous!

Your turn ...

What do your actions say about how you *truly* feel about yourself?

Are you silently at war with your body?

Does your meat suit define you?

Does your weight or body shape define or hold power over you?

Does your beauty (or perceived lack of beauty) define you?

Does your age define you?

Do the roles of your life define you?

Or, do YOU define you?

You have the power, Gorgeous ...

For an exercise designed to help you let go of programming that has you defining your value and worth by the age, size, weight and/ or beauty of your meat suit, please turn to pages 132 & 147-150.

FUNdamental Truth Four
The way you animate yourself and your life is integral to your authentic sexy.

Authentic Sexy Can Only Be Expressed When You Are In Alignment With Your Values and Beliefs.

s we've already explored, your external body – your meat suit – serves its purpose. However, it's what's inside that *really* matters.

You can demonstrate what's inside of you by the way you animate yourself and your life.

This means what you do.

Your actions.

Your thoughts.

Your words.

The way you live your life.

Specifically, do you live with integrity?

Do your thoughts match your values and actions?

Do your actions match your words?

Do you speak your Truth?

In other words …

Do you *own* your life?

I am going to reframe that last question by asking:

Can you imagine how you would feel on your death bed *knowing* that you held back?

To know that you didn't live fully?

I'm going to take a wild guess and say that you'd wish you could do it all again.

What I am trying to say here is that you only have one life to live in the body you are in. Why not learn how to celebrate it?

Why not learn how to dance with it?

Why not be sexy on your own terms … while you still have time?

Why not embody sexy in ways that both honor and value your worth?

In ways that make your heart sing.

It IS possible.

Seriously.

There is no time like NOW to dust off your sexy and marry it with your authenticity.

And, as is true with most things in life, if you want your world to shine with all shades of confidence and sexy, you have to do the work!

In this case "the work" is giving yourself permission to let go.

Let go of beliefs and values that are not yours and do not serve you.

Let go of ways of being you borrowed and still carry with you today, *even though* you have outgrown them.

LET GO so you have the *space* to welcome in the new.

Essentially, authentic animation of your life - and of sexy - begins and ends with you.

You get to choose how you animate yourself – which is based on your authentic values and beliefs – so that you can unleash and shine the REAL YOU to the world, in all your incredible, beautiful and GORGEOUS glory.

Now that's what I call sexy!

For exercises designed to help you explore your authentic animation needs, please go to pages 154-156, 159 - 160.

In order to tap into your
authentic sensual nature
- as defined by you -
you may have to UNlearn
and/or reprogram some of your
previously held beliefs,
like how you view
your body,
the concept of sexy
or yourself, as a sensual being.

FUNdamental Truth Five:
Being authentically sexy means taking responsibility.

*You Are The Only One Who Can
Live Your Life. No One Can
Do It For You.*

I n this culture, many people use the lenses of society's status quos to influence how they view themselves.

Specifically, they blindly allow media, books, movies, their faith, family, peer groups, government, school systems, corporations and more dictate what they believe, which is then what they base their decisions and actions on.

Most people have perfected the **herd mentality** and conduct themselves accordingly.

In fact, it seems as though most don't realize that they have a choice to decide for themselves what they do or don't buy into.

Somehow they seem to have forgotten that, even though they are part of something incredible that is larger than them (society … and the universe), they are still individuals and have the right to *choose* how

Health Tip:
Shape shifting to fit into socially constructed boxes subtly teaches people that they are broken (because no one quite fits), which can lead people to not loving themselves (or allowing others to love them) as much as they deserve.

they define all aspects of their identity and life based on what is right for them, as unique human beings.

Instead, they hide their true nature (and value!) behind an image that is not theirs, based on views that do not truly belong to them, believing that if they just "do it right" and play by the rules they will be "safe."

Fit in.

Be liked.

Become "worthy" by earning someone's love.

This disconnection from their authentic self locks them inside carefully constructed armor so that they end up alone in a "cage" that they created for themselves.

Inside this cage they end up marching their life to a beat that does not resonate with them or allow them to move through life with joy and ease.

They've learned to "paint inside the lines" and do everything they were told to do to be happy.

They've pursued what they've been told to pursue.

Read what they've been told to read.

Acquired "the" job and "the" car and all the "stuff" they have been told to have.

And yet, most still experience quiet unrest.

They feel less than fulfilled.

Less than full of life.

And they are confused because *even though* they were "doing it right" for some reason they've never been truly happy.

For some reason, *even though* they've "gone through the motions" to make it look like they live the "perfect" and ideal life, they've never had what they truly want.

Therefore, they feel stuck.

In a cage.

Constricted.

And confined.

Deep down they know that they have outgrown the cage they have been living in ...

They are aware that something inside of them is waking up and wants to be set FREE!

But, they don't know how to become free.

There are no rules for how to disconnect from the unrest.

What do they do and/or say when there is no script to follow?

What do they do and/or say if and/or when they choose to leave the herd?

The Truth is that the answer is simple.

All they have to do is take responsibility.

That's right.

They take responsibility for the ways they animate their life so that they can express themselves in ways that feel great to them.

They take responsibility so they can finally kick their inner victim (or broken self views) to the curb so their authentic inner *and* outer gorgeous gal can come out to play.

They also take responsibility so they can choose to define sexy for themselves and stand tall as a self-defined authentically sexy creature.

Because they know that when they express their lives through the power of authentic sexy, they can't help but feel happier, more confident, vibrant, **alive** and, of course, deliciously sexy.

Powerful Truth:
If we don't take
responsibility, we
don't step into our power.

So, how about it, Gorgeous?

Are you ready to take responsibility for your sexy and express gorgeous, delicious you on your own terms?

In ways that nourish and empower you and your life?

After all, you are the only person who can define authentic sexy for you.

For an exercise to help you gain clarity around where you need to take responsibility, gain balance and live your life on your terms, please go to page 156.

Taking responsibility for both how you view *and* feel about your age, body, beauty and life is a powerful way to live because it means you are living *your* life on *your* terms.

FUNdamental Truth Six:
It's up to you to define your authentic sexy.

Other People's Values, Morals, Opinions
and Ideas About "Sexy" Do Not Belong To You.
Therefore, They Are Not Yours To Carry.
Unless You Want To.

In this culture we sing a child's song about rubber and glue bouncing off me and sticking to you. However, in my youth, I never acknowledged the underlying Truth of these lyrics.

With that being said, as an adult, I greatly appreciate this "Rubber and Glue" philosophy because it serves to remind me of the Truth. When people share their thoughts and/or try to impose their beliefs or ideals onto me I remember:

a) It's not personal,
b) It's their opinion,
and therefore
c) It's not *my* baggage to carry.

Real Life Example:

For many years, I felt like someone was looking at me and judging if I was explicitly sexy.

I really didn't like that; I felt I had to shrink when I wanted to unleash the sexy side of myself!

Thus, in order to stop feeling uncomfortable, I learned how to **tent** my sexy circus and shut down that side of myself in certain circumstances.

Other times, I'd purposely not allow myself to look as gorgeous outside as I felt inside because I was well aware of how "gorgeous gals" are viewed in this society.

(In other words, I'd allow myself to be psuedo-gorgeous but never truly gorgeous - meaning deliciously, fully expressed gorgeous, as defined by me).

Why?

Because I didn't feel confident enough to proudly shine my beautiful and/or sexy sides wherever I pleased.

Besides, I didn't want to suffer the consequences of touching someone else's insecurity.

(You and I both know how painful the judgmental wrath of other women can be. Being vilified or ostracized is never fun.)

Health Tip:
When we take things personally they become ours and, in turn, go into our backpacks. However, when we objectively examine what feels right and best for us, we take the first step towards freeing ourselves from the burden of someone else's reality.

However, thanks to understanding the Rubber and Glue philosophy, it became much easier for me to take responsibility and feel both safe enough and confident enough to be me whenever and wherever I pleased.

In other words, I *now know* that others' views of me do not belong to me and therefore I don't have to carry them.

Daily Thought To Self:
The only thing I know for certain is this: I have this moment,
right now. So I am going to let my Freak Flag fly high. If
someone has a problem with me being me, that burden is
theirs alone to carry. Besides, I am going to make sure I am
too busy having fun and living my life to the fullest to notice!

Now let's apply this to *your* life ...

Does it feel good to carry other people's limits, beliefs, values
and perceptions of sexy, beauty and desirability with you, as if
you own them?

Filling your mental and emotional backpack with heavy baggage that weighs you down and challenges you to live your life
in ways that feels good to you. (*Especially when* you are not guaran-
teed tomorrow!)

However, what if you could choose to remove your ill fitting backpack and leave it on the side of the road of your life?

Are you ready to let go of how you think you should be?

How you think sexy should look, move and talk?

What age and size sexy should be?

Are you ready to *redefine sexy* so it feels good to you?

I bet you will be surprised by what you discover.

In fact, I already know that your authentic sexy is a million times
more delicious than the "you" you are when you hide your light behind other's views of what is right and wrong; behind other's views
of what is sexy.

How are you feeling, Beautiful?

Are you ready to redefine sexy to fit *your* views,
ideas, values and life?

Isn't it exciting to know that it *is* possible?

Not only because YOUR version of sexy will feel incredibly
delicious and nourishing to you.

But also because you have defined sexy for yourself,
which means you can only get it right!

Sexy Tip:

Emotional and psychological boundaries are necessary for personal happiness and mental health. Imagine yourself like a peach: sweet, nourishing and incredibly **juicy**. The REAL YOU is delicious, while having a strong seed at the core. Others' views and opinions are not permitted to make it past the outer layer - the flesh. Therefore, you have the choice to let ideas and views in, or not. If other's ideas or views don't resonate with you and/or if they do not help your seed-self grow, you have the choice to dismiss them and replace them with views and opinions that nourish you. You have the power.

Caution:

The opposite is also true. Your core needs to house positive self images so you know that you are worthy of happiness and so that you don't take other's ideas of life and/or you personally. If your core is rotten with anger or self doubt, you will not be protected from other's negative views because you will see those views as validating your own rather than for what they are -nonsense. By redefining sexy to fit your curves, age, personality and life you are able to protect your mental, emotional and even physical health because you are confident enough to know – on a DNA/cellular level – that it is safe for you to shine and be seen for who you really are: a miraculous, unrepeatable, authentically sexy creature.

For an exercise to subjectively examine what feels right and best for you, please turn to pages 117-118.

Reality Check:
It's much easier to bury yourself underneath someone else's
"reality" and numb yourself to *your* Truth.

So much historical, religious and social judgment surrounds
sexuality and sexual ways of being; it's no wonder it's
challenging to decipher up from down and/or left from right.

As if there is a "right" or "wrong" way to be authentic. *As if*
someone else can choreograph your unique **sensual groove** and
expression of authentic sexy.

After all, sexy is not that serious.
Being happy and feeling delicious while you are still alive and
able to enjoy life – now that *is* serious.

FUNdamental Truth Seven:
You can only get sexy RIGHT.

---

*"What would you attempt to do if you knew
you could not fail?"* Dr. Robert Schuller

YOU

CANNOT

NOT

GET

AUTHENTIC

SEXY

RIGHT!

Seriously!

Why?

Because the simple truth is that sexy is malleable.

Additionally, the process of *redefining sexy* involves eliminating labels like "right" and "wrong."

And redefining sexy is paramount to the UNlearning process.

By letting go of defining sexy as something complicated with unclear rules and conditions, you open yourself up to a NEW way of thinking.

It is also because of this letting go of labels that makes it possible for you to not have to get sexy "right" (meaning comparing *your* expression of sexy to an ill defined and impossible to embody expression of sexy).

When you disconnect from the idea that sexy is "serious" (meaning important – as in a measure of your value and worth) and acknowledge that your authentic sexy is a joyful, empowering, and confident expression of your authentic self, sexy becomes easy to "get right" because it is defined by you!

How many times in your life have you been told that something that can seem so complex, like sexy, is actually something you cannot – in any way, shape or form – get wrong?

Let's pause with that thought for a moment so that it can really sink in ...

That's right; you AS YOU *already* ARE authentically sexy.

And all you have to do to step into that fact is just BE!

I'm going to substantiate this new paradigm by tying it into current trends within the Personal Development Industry. Specifically, the concepts of "being present" and "being authentic".

Pop culture examples of being authentic include:
- Our culture's obsession with reality television shows, which demonstrates our fascination with "real" or authentic people and the lives they lead.
- Countless shelves of self-help books both encouraging and/ or teaching people how to become more authentic.
- Countless spiritual/life/self-help workshops and live events that encourage awakening and provide frameworks for people to live more purposeful and authentic lives.

Pop culture examples of being present include:
- Books such as "The Power of Now" by Ekhart Tolle[1];
- Countless quotes by Oprah Winfrey (that reflect the content of her powerful show) including:

"Breathe. Let go. And remind yourself that this very moment is the only one you know you have for sure."[2] *Oprah Winfrey.*
- Teachings within yoga and meditation classes - both of which are extremely popular in today's culture.

Linking these aspects together creates the framework for authentic sexy, as the roots of authentic sexy extend from both personal authenticity and living one's life within the moment.

"Meditation is
essential - like
vitamins and water."
Tara Antler[3], Meditation Expert

Powerful Thought:
Uncomplicating sexy by
allowing it to just BE is
the key to authentic sexy.

Okay Beautiful, are you willing to step into the present
moment and heal the relationship you have with your
body and, in turn, your life?

Are you ready to *allow yourself to just be* so that you can
experience the Truth - that you *are good enough* and
worthy of all things good - as you are, right now?

After all, authentic sexy is not complicated ... all you
have to do is be you!

Question:
Both you and I know that you are an EXPERT at
judging yourself. However, what would happen if you
let go of judgement and redefined sexy to fit you?
How much extra time and energy would you
have when you allow yourself to just be?

For an exercise designed to help you FILL the time you free up by
allowing yourself to "just be," please turn to pages 172.

NOTES

1 Tolle, E. (1997). *The Power of now: A guide to spiritual enlightenment* . Vancouver: Namaste.

2 Winfrey, O. (2002). What Oprah knows for sure about letting it all go. Retrieved from http://www.oprah.com/spirit/What-Oprah-Knows-for-Sure-About-Letting-It-All-Go

3 Tara Antler
http://www.tarahealingsanctuary.com

FUNdamental Truth Eight:
Authentic vulnerability is a powerful strength.

---

*It Takes A Lot Of Strength To Lay
Down Your Armor And Be Seen
For Who You Really Are.*

When I discuss the topics of authenticity and strength within my workshops, most women have no idea what I am talking about because their views of strength tend to be grounded in the old paradigm of "**strong**."

In fact, many women have shared that they feel powerful *because* they are "strong." They explain that being "strong" makes them feel fiercely independent and able to overcome any obstacle that gets in the way of their dreams and aspirations.

In many circumstances, this type of "strength" is an excellent developmental strategy because it enables them to successfully take on the duties of modern life – in their own ways and on their own terms.

However, by *only* embodying "strength," many women have become disconnected from their **authentic strength.**

(In my workshops, this is where most women have the tendency to lean in, as the discussion of this concept is oftentimes very new to them).

The fact is this: a woman can *also* be incredibly powerful when she steps into what has always been viewed as weakness within the old paradigm of "strength."

In other words, it is possible for a woman to be powerful - *even when* she opens herself up to being authentically vulnerable.

Let's pause with this thought for a moment.

That's right.

A woman can be powerful and live her dreams *even when* she has laid down her armor to stand "naked" within her authentic vulnerability.

> "True strength comes from standing tall in your Truth without feeling the need to justify it."
>
> *Josephine Auciello*[1]

In other words, it's not authentic for a woman to be "strong" all the time.

My research substantiates this point. Many women have reported feeling that their perceived need to be "strong" all the time makes them feel trapped and unable to *truly* be themselves.

The lived manifestation of this embodiment of "strong" is women hiding their true nature by monitoring their social appearances so that their images fit within (perceived and real) social norms.

They shape shift their personalities, don social masks, and employ methods of social engagement that are meant to suit their immediate circumstances but do not reflect their authentic nature.

Again, a positive feature in some circumstances, but not a sustainable way of being for an optimal quality of life.

In fact, many women from my workshops have reported that always being "strong" challenges their mental and emotional health, not only because they feel disconnected from other people as a result of the masks they wear, but also because they are so used to being "strong" that they sometimes feel as though they are carrying the weight of the world on their shoulders!

> The muscle of vulnerability must be exercised in order to strip away the many layers of armor that have been constructed to perpetuate "strength."

In fact, many report that they are unsure of where to turn for help if and when the burden of inauthentic strength – and all the ties that bind them to that - begin to crush them.

The fact is this: it takes a lot of "strength" to hide your light to fit inside the box of social norms.

In this case, the box is the old paradigm that expects women to be "strong."

However, true strength is not hiding.

It's also not draining or heavy but rather engaging, inspiring and uplifting!

Darling, I think it is time someone asked you the question …

ARE YOU TIRED OF BEING "STRONG" YET?

Aren't you tired of wearing your "strong" mask and hiding incredible, miraculous, authentic you?

Are you ready to just be?

And maybe not wear make up to the grocery store?

Because you can.

Because you ARE totally pretty enough!

Or, perhaps wear your hot pink stilettos to pick your son up from his Little League game?

Because you can.

Because you don't have to stop being sexy – in ways that make you feel good – just because you are a mom.

Or, maybe speak your Truth?

Because you can.

Because your voice deserves to be heard.

And, because when you are coming from an authentically strong place, you are safe to say how you really feel and what you are *really thinking* ...

This may mean honoring you and your voice by speaking your Truth *even when* you believe other people may not want to hear it.

Or, it may mean walking away from arguments before you say something you don't mean.

Or, it may mean acknowledging that you need help and inviting someone to share your load. (Especially because you do so much for others all the time!)

By the way, it's okay if you are not able to carry the weight of the world. No one but you is expecting you to ...

The Truth is, authentic strength takes courage.

It means laying down your armor and being exposed for all the deliciousness that you are.

In other words, you can be "strong" or you can be real.

And I believe being real is an incredibly kind way of being.

> Kindness is incredibly sexy.

Real Life Example:

I was dating a gentleman a couple of years ago. I was newly single and met him on an online dating site. He was very attractive and we discovered we had a lot in common. We chatted for several weeks before meeting up. When the time to meet came, I was very excited but kept in mind warnings from friends about online dating – sometimes the individual you meet online is not always who you meet in person.

After our first date I started to develop a MONSTER CRUSH on this guy. He totally blew my mind. He was what I saw and more! A complete gentleman (and an exceptionally good make-out partner!). We dated for several weeks and then all of a sudden, POOF!

He vanished, which left me confused.

He "went dark" on me, as in disconnected and stopped communicating for a few (long) days. When he finally did reach out, via email, he told me he didn't think it would work out between us because he saw me as someone who was "not open enough."

This shocked and surprised me because I saw myself as completely open. (However, being completely honest, at that point in my life I was only completely open with my friends. He was still "on trial").

My **ego** was mad because he called me out for not keeping it 100% real with him. (By the way, my authentic self LOVED that he could tell! I also love that he would have been more attracted to the "real" me versus the ½ real me).

Anyways, by the time he messaged me and told me his thoughts, my monkey mind had already spun my heart into feelings of hurt and rejection. In fact, I had constructed emotional armor to protect myself from him while he went dark.

Therefore, after receiving his email I decided I couldn't be bothered to tell him my side of the story, which was that he was traveling pretty much the entire time we were dating (how open can someone really get online and via text?), and that I was scared to be completely vulnerable (right away) with someone I met on an online dating site - especially after the warnings of my friends.

After reflecting on that experience, I realized that in the interaction with this man I let my ego as well as my perceptions of who I thought I "should be" hold power over me. In doing so, I accidentally disconnected myself from my authentic, powerful and loving self.

(MASSIVE **interpersonal fail!**)

Regardless, I was able to grow so much because he was honest with me.

He highlighted a flaw, which in turn allowed me to work deeply on myself.

His gift of honesty triggered the activation of innate tools that I had forgotten I had within me.

His honesty *reminded me* that I am safe to be the real me all the time – regardless of how I met someone or how long I've known them.

In other words, this experience taught me how deeply I was socialized to be a certain way versus being authentic.

I knew then and there that I had to work hard at learning how to harness the courage to stand up and be seen for who I really am – even when it feels uncomfortable and/or awkward.

This experience made me see that by not being 100% me, my life was not progressing the way I wanted. In fact, I was putting myself in a cage that did not fit my authentic self - and I was not okay with that!

At that point in my life I had yet to discover that when I have the courage and authentic strength to follow my heart (also known as my authentic self or my Truth), I always make the best decisions for me.

Sure, following my Truth may feel uncomfortable sometimes (because my brain doesn't understand what is going on), but at least I can be confident in *knowing* - on a DNA/cellular level - that I am always safe.

In fact, I've found it is actually impossible for me to get hurt when I follow its guidance. (This is probably a scary truth if you have never experienced it before).

Thankfully, as a result of this experience, I have learned to be 100% me all the time; *even when* it feels weird; *even when* I feel uncomfortable.

Thankfully, the fruits of this work show up in all my relationships now – even here on these pages.

How delicious!

And if I can do it ... anyone can do it!

> Getting comfortable with being uncomfortable is a gateway to authentic sexy.

To conclude this new perspective on "strength" vs. authentic strength, I recognize that it is a fascinating irony that a woman's greatest capacity for strength comes from an old paradigm's definition of weakness.

I also recognize that it is fitting to explore the Truth of authentic strength now that we are deconstructing old paradigms and creating new, empowering ones.

So, how about it, Gorgeous?

Are you ready to be authentically strong and stand up as YOU?

Delicious, courageous, lovable, miraculous, unrepeatable and incredible YOU.

The New Paradigm

Strong = Vulnerable
Vulnerable = Authentic
Authentic = Sexy

Expert View:

"Being authentic can conjure up deep issues around self worth, rejection, and visibility. It can also bring up feelings of shame and insecurity born in past experiences, which have undoubtedly left scars. These scars often get triggered when trying to be your authentic self. However, it is at that very moment that your greatest opportunity for personal growth exists because it provides you with the opportunity to unveil your greatest strength: your vulnerability."

Joesphine Auciello[1], author & femininity expert

For an exercise designed to help you take the first step towards finding the courage to move past fears surrounding letting go of being "strong" (or other outdated ways of being) so that you can step into NEW, juicer ways of living life, please turn to page 113.

NOTES

1 Josephine Auciello, Author & Feminine Essence Expert
http://www.femininebodywisdom.com

FUNdamental Truth Nine:
Laying down your mask is incredibly sexy.

Authentic Sexy Wears No Mask. She Is Safe.
Her Authentic Confidence And Strength
Protect Her.

uthentic sexy is as delicious in sweatpants as it is in glamorous apparel.

Without redefining sexy, this statement may seem absurd. However, it is the Truth.

In a nutshell, "sexy" (as in if you do "this," wear this, have this, fit into this, have this size breasts, etc. you are sexy) is a mask, which means there *is* a time and place for expression.

Defining sexy by old parameters means there *is* a right and wrong way.

Whereas, *authentic sexy* knows no bounds.

In other words, authentic sexy always expresses itself exactly how it wants to be expressed.

Classy,

Sassy,

Provocative,

Assertive,

Kind,

Subtle,

Demanding,

Coy ...

Authentic sexy is unique to you; *your* way of being; *your* state of mind; *your* expression of gorgeous you.

When you remove the "mask of sexy" (or whatever mask you wear) your authentic sexy is able to come to life.

Additionally, as you begin to own your authentic sexy, you will discover the boundaries dissolving of when and where you previously believed sexy "should" exist.

With this new view, all areas of your life become infused with deliciousness.

You begin to feel as you have always deserved to feel – confident, vibrant, happy and, of course, incredibly sexy!

However, before this can occur, you have to learn how to let your authentic sexy *flow through you*; meaning your "self" will have to step aside.

The "self" I am referring to is the image or mask you have carefully constructed of yourself and work very hard to maintain.

You know, your (pick whichever one(s) resonates with you):

"sexy",

"good girl",

"smart girl",

or "bad girl" image.

The "I want to be taken seriously" façade,

the "I'm a mom (or, I'm too old), therefore I cannot be sexy" lie,

or the "I don't want to be judged, so I will just tow-the-line and hope no one notices me" experience.

Yes, I know you hide in those places.

Thought you were alone?

You're not.

Many women hide in the same corners as you.

In fact, we all pretend and have different personas that we expose, depending on who is around, what our perceived expectations are in a particular group, and/or the social roles that are common in a particular situation.

The unfortunate Truth is that by wearing a mask we miss out on some very delicious aspects of life.

In fact, most masks we wear are outdated, and by unconsciously wearing them we inadvertently allow the continuation of social roles and scripts that no longer serve us, as women, and in turn, as a society.

I'm sorry. Please don't be offended...

I recognize there has been significant progress for women.

Women are allowed to vote.

Women are allowed to work outside the home.

Women are allowed to take pole dancing classes and, in a contained environment, flaunt a delicious, albeit hidden aspect of their human experience – their authentic sexy – for the five or ten women there.

However, HEAVEN FORBID that that same woman flaunt her authentic sexy at a bar or at her staff Christmas party with her partner/husband/coworkers present!

Because what would people think?!? How would she be viewed?

I know you are thinking it, so I am going to say it. She would be judged.

Or, more specifically, she would be fearful of being perceived in a negative or socially inappropriate light.

Understandably, this fear provides powerful motivation to NOT engage sexy - authentic or not!

However, by shape shifting ourselves and donning masks that do not reflect our true, powerful nature simply because it has always been done that way has ended up doing us a great disservice!

Why?

Because every single woman is an aunt, friend, sister, lover, mother, confidant, daughter and/or more for someone, somewhere.

And, I can confidently guess that, of the roles previously listed, women are expressing one or more aspects of their authentic nature, which means that their masks are off and their beautiful, feminine, sensual nature is shining through.

Which, as you know, IS a woman's expression of authentic sexy.

Are you starting to see how sexy *really isn't* that serious?

That it *really isn't* what we've been trained to believe it to be?

Therefore, is it rational to think that the people who really "see" us are going to get upset if we "let loose" and be our beautiful, authentically sexy selves - anywhere we please?

I doubt it. After all, authentic sexy isn't a negative expression.

It shouldn't be something to feel shame about.

In fact, authentic sexy is nurturing, kind, beautiful and intelligent.

So, why hide it?!?

It's an absolute gift to the world!

In fact, my guess is that anyone who has ever seen *your* authentic and amazing sides LOVE it and think it's absolutely BEAUTIFUL!

Yes?

... Or,

YES!

Powerful Truth:
Your people don't stuff you into a box.
You choose to do that yourself!

In fact, these people likely REJOICE when you give yourself permission to let your hair down and be the real you due to the powerful ripple effect that happens when you are authentic.

Why?

Because when you allow yourself to be the real you, other people will feel safe enough to be the **real them.**

And I don't know about you, but to me, life doesn't get much more delicious than that!

Authentic people are deliciously sexy!

Example:

Not to toot my own horn but I know I am sexy, on a DNA/cellular level.

However, *even I* have stopped myself from being me and oozing my particular brand of sexy-deliciousness because I KNEW how people could perceive me.

I had this brilliant AH-HA! moment in Mexico.

I was feeling quite saucy on tequila, dancing the night away with some Yukon buddies and found myself on the bar top shakin' my groove thang. I sobered up instantly when I recognized myself doing one of my signature sensual groove dance moves – a delicious and empowering way I like to express my authentic sexy.

GASP!

I was in PUBLIC!

I reprimanded myself for taking off my "mask" and letting my inner sexy come out to play. After all, I was in public and I did not want to be perceived as "that girl."

Thankfully, in the next breath I realized that my sexy self is a very real and authentic part of who I am as a human being. I realized that if I chose to NOT let that beautiful side of me shine then I would be robbing the world of my spectacular **heart light.**

... And who am I to do that?!?

The world needs me.

Just like it needs you.

In fact, it's your responsibility to shine your light to the world.

One way to do this is by taking off your mask(s).

The reason I am sharing this story with you is because I am SURE some part of you is worried about letting your authentic sexy self come out to play. You want to be taken seriously at work or by your partner or ... ???

I acknowledge that our society has conditioned us so well that we still, on some level, discount women who choose to disregard the "rules" and own their sexy anytime and anywhere they like.

However, as we have been examining this entire book, "sexy" is a lot broader than traditional views of the concept.

In fact, sexy is accessible to everyone.

It is defined *by* the individual *for* the individual.

Therefore, it is impossible to get it wrong AND impossible for it to be "bad."

In other words, it IS possible for you to be sexy, taken seriously AND be everything you came here to this planet to be.

And you can do it all on your own terms.

You just have to give yourself permission to go for it!

In other words, take off your mask and just be.

Be beautiful, authentically sexy you.

Mask Removal: A Case Study

One of my clients was called a slut in high school simply because she had big boobs.

She was really hurt by the name calling because she knew she wasn't a slut (based on the traditional meaning of the word, as compared with her actions).

In an effort to show everyone her Truth, she donned a "good girl" mask and worked hard to be viewed as a good, pure girl. It was her goal to be seen as un-sexual as possible.

The reward for her efforts was disconnection from her sensuality.

In fact, she came to me with no idea how to express herself as an authentic sexual being.

During our time together, she discovered that being a "good girl" didn't feel right to her. In fact, it was causing friction – not only inside of her but also within her sexual relationship with her husband!

Can you see how this client was disconnected from her authenticity by wearing a mask she constructed to protect herself?

The truth is that she is a strong, authentic, powerfully sexy woman but wearing the mask of "good girl" kept her stuck in a painful pattern that started in her youth.

However, through our work together she took her power back by giving herself permission to re-frame her view of sexy to fit her adult life.

She now reports major quality of life improvements.

1) She has finally healed her relationship with her body and now feels confident to stand tall as the sexy woman she is - on her own terms.

2) She enjoys a deeper sexual relationship with her husband.

Essentially, after learning how to find and express her unique and genuine expression of sexy, she no longer feels the need to hide her body, beauty or curve appeal.

She has learned - right down to her DNA - that her body doesn't define her ... but rather SHE defines her!

And her reward?

A gigantic boost in her quality of life!

A Question For You, Sexy:

What parts of you do you squash and work hard to hide because you think they won't meet people's approval and/or will put you in a position to be judged?

For an exercise designed to help you explore the (unconscious) masks you wear in your life, please turn to page 164.

Recap:
Truth 1: Trying to be sexy (by wearing a mask)
is not sexy.
Truth 2: You being YOU is SEXY.
Truth 3: Being authentically sexy is not "bad"
(because it's not *that* serious and refer to # 2)

FUNdamental Truth Ten
Sexy is synonymous with confidence.

Authentic Sexy Is A State Of Mind.

S exy is not about how you look. It's about who you are and how you feel.

In fact, authentic sexy is a state of mind.

What most people don't realize is that the true deliciousness that infuses sexy has very little to do with the way you look, your body size, your breast size, your job, your hair length or if you fit into socially prescribed views of "sexy."

In fact, you don't even have to define yourself as sexy to be authentically sexy!

Why?

Because it's not *that* serious!

It's true!

It's possible for you to feel sexy no matter what.

… even if you have small breasts;

… even if you have big breasts;

... even if you are a mom;

... even if you are not a mom;

... even if you weigh more than you would like;

... even if you weigh less than you would like;

... even if you are taller than most;

... even if you are shorter than most;

... even if you have mobility, visibility, or hearing issues;

... even if you are 100% able-bodied;

... even if you feel insecure about having extra body or facial hair;

... even if you are a grooming pro or hairless wonder;

... even if you are divorced;

... even if you are married;

... even if you are single;

... even if you have survived cancer or another life threatening illness that may have altered your physical form or emotional, spiritual or psychological landscape;

... even if you have vagina shame, think your vagina smells[1] and/or you feel insecure about the size of your labia[2];

---

1 Make sure to clean the folds of your vagina thoroughly with a mild cleanser. To clean the clitoris, try using a moistened Q-Tip to gently clean out the hood. If, after cleansing your vagina thoroughly, you still have an odor, please see your physician.
2. Your labia are perfect. Period.

That's right!

... *EVEN IF* you think it's utterly impossible for you to be sexy!

Because the fact of the matter is this: sexy is synonymous with confidence.

Confidence: A Snap Shot

In university I went to a strip club to watch an amateur contest - a competition where non-professional strippers take off their clothes on stage in front of a live audience to win a large cash prize. That evening, one of the contestants was a large black woman. (I would guess her weight was approximately 300 pounds). Understandably, there was a buzz in the club because a woman of that size was not the typical contestant in those types of events - at least not in south eastern Ontario. Regardless, when the time for her show came, she crawled like a cat onto the stage and put on such a spectacular show that she ended up winning the competition - much to the surprise and delight of all in attendance!

This example demonstrates – in no uncertain terms – that sexy is synonymous with confidence and has very little to do with the socially prescribed notion of what sexy is "supposed" to look like.

For an exercise designed to help you understand - on a DNA/cellular level - that you are delicious and authentically sexy, as you are right now (which will boost your confidence immediately), please turn to page 123 & 127.

Side Note:
It is a natural process of maturity to gain
confidence regarding your body and
sexuality as you age. For example,
sexy may not feel the same or have
the same meaning at ages 25, 35 or 65.
This idea supports that *authentic sexy* matures
with you and is a dynamic expression of life
instead of being a rigid concept.
By learning that sexy is both not that
serious and completely redefinable, you
open yourself up to a lifetime of experiencing
greater happiness, better relationships, more
satisfying sexual relations, a higher sense of self
worth, an improved relationship with your body, as
well as so much more.

CHAPTER FIVE:
Lessons to help uncover and unleash your authentic sexy.

"Be here now.
You can be somewhere else later."
My mom

In the land of deliciousness – where your authentic sexy lives - you are reminded to be here now.

Because by being here now, it doesn't serve you to judge the unfolding of the moment.

It also doesn't serve you to have any attachments to past conditioning.

You may, however, be able to feel the remnants of certain **shackles** tying you to useless and possibly unkind ways of thinking about your age, beauty, desirability and/or your body.

However, I am here to gently remind you that you (and you alone) hold the key to the shackles that renders your authentic sexy – your experience of visibility, personal value, worth and esteem - paralyzed.

Please listen closely, sweethear because I am going to tell you a secret ...

I know that there is a door available to you that you do not even know exists ... yet.

I know this is a bold statement. However, it is genuine feedback I have received from past clients. They told me they experienced a new world of deliciousness they didn't know they had access to prior to playing with me.

Knowing this, it is my honor and privilege to pay it forward.

I am thrilled to be your personal tour guide and to help you along this journey as you figure out how to release your YUM!

What I will need from you in return is your trust and your commitment to doing all the exercises in this chapter at the pace that feels authentic to you.

After all, the only way you can discover and unleash your authentic sensual nature – the essence of your authentic sexy – is to dive right in and explore it.

Please note: all of the exercises have been designed to engage you in both traditional *and* unusual ways. The intention is for you to create a personalized definition of authentic sexy that fits you unequivocally, which will help you step into NEW levels of confidence and personal power. Please keep in mind that you cannot get any of these exercises "wrong."

Enjoy!

Lesson One:
Learning something new can feel AwKwArD!

Step Outside Your "Known-Zone"
And Experience Your Authentic Sexy!

I am sure you have many skills that you are incredibly good at.

Cooking.

Baking.

Working.

Being a mom.

(---fill in the blank---)

However, *it is* human nature to forget about the learning curve that is necessary to become good at something new.

It's easy to forget that the first few steps can feel excruciatingly painful and be filled with frustration, negative feelings and not much humor.

The key is to remember that learning something new is really not *that* serious.

It's okay to be "bad" at something before you become good at it.

In fact, learning new things become easier when we give ourselves permission to be novice because it provides us with the safety and courage we need in order to take the first step.

Example:

I was in the first year of my nursing degree and I had to learn how to teach someone various skills, including: how to walk with a cane, make a bed complete with "nurse's corners," give a bed bath, and change bed sheets with a patient still in the bed.

I was being tested on these skills the following week. My homework was to learn all these skills because the test would be a random selection of one of them.

I took some time that weekend to practice on my brother and can remember thinking, "Getting someone to walk with a cane, easy peazy!"

But then I tried it. And here's what happened:

My brother was sitting on the couch and I stood in front of him, pretending he was my patient.

It was in that moment that something strange happened. My mouth went dry. My heart rate accelerated. My body was physically responding to the stress I was psychologically and emotionally experiencing[1]!

As I tried to teach him how to use a broom as his cane, I couldn't figure out how to make my mouth form the words to explain the simple task to him.

I was so aWkWaRd, which shocked me!

Typically, I am excellent at the things I choose to do. Therefore, it was astonishing to me that I had the capability to be miles less than perfect at something – especially something so seemingly easy!

Thankfully, I found a way to recognize that I didn't need to be "perfect" and gave myself permission to try. With this, my "fear paralysis" subsided and it dawned on me that the task I wanted to accomplish was neither that hard nor that serious.

Thankfully, after a couple of practice runs, I found my words and was able to explain the task to my brother with ease.

Recap: by giving myself permission to not be 100% perfect (at first) allowed me the space to experience the growing pains of learning, which eventually enabled me to ace the exam.

Chances are you are not as silly as I am by thinking you need to be perfect at *everything*. However, I am sharing this story with you just in case you're like me and sometimes forget that learning something new can feel incredibly awkward and uncomfortable at first.

Exercise:
Using your non-dominant hand write the following
phrase fifty (50) times:
"I love you."
Give yourself permission to write poorly as you gain
the coordination necessary for this task.
Watch how your skills improve with practice and celebrate
your success! When you are finished, give yourself a
moment to acknowledge your courage for stepping outside
your "Known-Zone" and trying something new.

Reminder:

If, during your journey through this book experience, fear
begins to overtake you and tries to trick you into running
away, hiding, and/or surrendering to feeling "scared"
(meaning you are not physically in danger but you can
feel the fear that comes with stepping into new territory) ...
KEEP GOING!

You are going the right way!

The gift and treasure of your authentic
sexy is on the other side.

NOTES

1 University of Maryland Medical Centre. (2012, December
      2). Stress: The body's response. Retrieved from http://www.
      umm.edu/patiented/articles/what_biological_effects_of_
      acute_stress_000031_2.htm

Lesson Two:
Listening to and following your YES! is sexy.

Listening To And Honoring Your YES!
Will Make You A Master Of Creating
The Delicious Life You Desire.

Y ou are the ONLY ONE who knows what is true for you.

No one else lives your life.

Wears your dresses.

Drives your car.

Eats your food.

Or laughs, cries or snores quite like you.

Essentially, if you plug and play your life to fit inside a mold that is not made to order for your gorgeous frame and life then, chances are, something feels "off" to you.

However, *it is* possible to feel "on," as in happy, confident, vibrant and exquisitely sexy on a DNA/cellular level - every day!

But how do you find this new way?

The answer is simple: you follow your YES!

What is your YES!?

It is the quiet and truthful whisperings of your heart.

They belong to only you and are 100% accurate for you and your life.

Essentially, no one else can define for you who you are as a sexual and sensual being. However, if you let them – they will. This is why it's important to listen to your YES! so you can take responsibility and engage with your authentic sexy on your own terms.

You can find your YES! via several different methods. I will discuss two here:

1) Learn how to hear the whisperings of your heart saying NO!
2) Learn how to hear the whisperings of your heart saying YES!

Method #1: Hearing Your Heart Say NO!

Can you think of any ways of being that you embody AND that feel uncomfortable, heavy, not true and/or stunting to your essence and true self?

This may be something you have never thought about.

However, I am willing to bet that there are several aspects of your life view that do not feel good to you.

This internal friction – marked by negative and/or uncomfortable emotions, sensations or similar – are critically important and are asking to be listened to because they indicate your NO!.

Unfortunately, we are usually culturally conditioned to suppress, neglect and/or ignore these types of emotions and sensations. However, by giving yourself permission to acknowledge them and the gifts they bring helps guide you to your YES!.

Recap: the internal friction you experience indicates
that your YES! is not that particular world view and/or
way of being.

Method #2: Hearing Your Heart Say YES!

Now that you know what YES! feels like by being aware of its opposite, let's explore the other ways you can find your YES!

On the next page is an activity to center you with your Truth – the
place where your YES! lives.

Activity To Find Your YES!

Find a comfortable spot.

You can be sitting, standing or lying down.

Place a hand on your abdomen and see if you can feel the rise and fall of your belly as you breathe.

As you start focusing on your breath, can you breathe space into your thoughts to quiet the busy-ness of your mind?

(It's okay if you find that your mind seems to always want to latch onto thoughts and ride them off into the sunset. A busy mind full of chatter is a very human quality indeed).

Whenever you notice any thoughts in your head while you are doing this exercise, be gentle to yourself.

Bring your awareness back to your hand rising and falling on your belly in time with the tempo of your breath.

Conscious breathing is a simple, yet challenging task.

The purpose is to quiet the busy-ness of your mind and create space in order to *hear* what your heart – your Truth – is saying to you.

The fact is, you already have all the answers inside of you.

If you can listen - and really *hear* what you are being told - you will always know what is best for you.

Quiet your mind and go within.

Just so you know, it will probably not be some big "ah-ha!" moment.

You probably won't hear the voice of a deity.

However, I bet you will meet someone there that you have encountered before.

You may never have known that that powerful part of you *IS* you and has a name: Your Authentic Self/your Truth/your Heart/your YES!.

Interestingly, the more you listen to this side of yourself, the more you will start to understand that everything really is as it should be, right now.

In other words, whatever you are experiencing in your life – regardless of whether you judge it as good, bad, hard, etc. – is actually *exactly* what you need to be experiencing right now in order to wake up, grow, become more joyful, vibrant, confident and, in turn, feel sexier.

Checking In:

How did this exercise feel?

Please know that as you get used to sitting within a present space (such as was just outlined in the previous exercise), your YES! will begin to appear faster and with greater ease.

Additionally, the more you experience your YES! (or your Truth), you will find that your sense of peace will begin to rise as your levels of anxiety and depression decrease.

This phenomenon occurs because you are creating the space for yourself to just be.

And inside the space of be-ing lives peace.

All of the answers you seek
can be found *INSIDE* of you.

Take a moment to pause
and go within.

Lesson Three:
Redefining sexy

You Are Not Broken.
Instead, It's The Concepts Of
Sexy And Desirability Within
This Culture That Are Broken.

To increase both a woman's health status and her quality of life, it's vital that she redefines sexy so that it is authentic to her.

Sexy can (and should!) fit her curves, age, personality and life.

To elaborate on this point, I am going to reiterate how views of a woman's body combined with the adage that "sex sells" have become staples in the social message diet we, as members of this society, are fed. Therefore, it has become very important for all women to be seen – or not seen – as sexy.

Because of this, sexy becomes *really serious.*

Sexy has rules.

Sexy is defined.

Sexy is good … sometimes.

Sexy is bad … other times.

Sexy is confusing.

But, what if sexy wasn't *that* serious?

What if sexy just is what it is – an aspect of one's humanity?

Moreover, what if a woman is able to maintain her *human rights* when she stands in her power as an authentically sexy creature?

Let's pause with that thought for a moment...

Powerful Thought:
A woman's human rights are challenged when she lives in fear of being labeled, ostracized, or made to fight for her worth for being (or not being) sexy.

How *powerful* if a woman can *finally* feel SAFE ENOUGH to stop engaging these unwritten and illusive rules.

How *delicious* if a woman can *finally* feel SAFE ENOUGH to be seen for who she really is: a delicious, beautiful, and feminine creature?

The sad truth is that this humongous issue is brushed under the metaphorical social rug to such an extent that women actually believe it's normal to experience deep unrest about their body/beauty/age/sexy.

In fact, the vast majority do not know that there is another way!

Thankfully, you and I know differently ...

On the next page is an exercise for you to re-frame your view of sexy so it's meaning can transform into a delicious way of being that can fit your age, curves, personality and life like your favorite little black dress.

Exercise:

Take a moment to imagine SEXY as the most delicious, positive, empowering force available to you, as a woman.

What would it look like?

How would it dress, feel and smile?

Would it be joyful, radiant, magnificent, or … ?

Is it friendly, kind, confident, magnetic, powerful abundant, natural, or … ?

Now that you have spent some time discovering an unbridled expression of sexy – the most delicious expression of sexy for you – turn the page and complete the next exercise.

Make a check mark beside each expression of authentic sexy that resonates with you.

In the spaces provided, write all the additional features that reflect your (you)nique concept of what sexy would be – if it could be anything you wanted it to be.

Please note: There are no "right" or "wrong" answers, simply authentic ones. Please use an additional piece of paper if you run out of writing space.

What Is Authentically Sexy To You?

1. Authentic sexy is the NEW expression of beautiful
2. Authentic sexy is the NEW wave to confidence
3. Authentic sexy is the NEW confident power
4. Authentic sexy is the NEW practice of peace
5. Authentic sexy is the NEW approach to vibrant health
6. Authentic sexy is the NEW direction of joy
7. Authentic sexy is the NEW route to peace
8. Authentic sexy is the NEW vein to magnificence
9. Authentic sexy is the NEW wave of feminine radiance
10. Authentic sexy is the NEW eruption of deliciousness
11. Authentic sexy is the NEW feminine power.
12. Authentic sexy is the NEW expression of power
13. Authentic sexy is the NEW realization of beauty
14. Authentic sexy is the NEW realization of power
15. Authentic sexy is the NEW expression of love
16. Authentic sexy is the NEW
17. Authentic sexy is the NEW
18. Authentic sexy is the NEW
19. Authentic sexy is the NEW
20. Authentic sexy is the NEW
21. Authentic sexy is the NEW
22. Authentic sexy is the NEW
23. Authentic sexy is the NEW
24. Authentic sexy is the NEW
25. Authentic sexy is the NEW
26. Authentic sexy is the NEW
27. Authentic sexy is the NEW
28. Authentic sexy is the NEW
29. Authentic sexy is the NEW
30. Authentic sexy is the NEW
31. Authentic sexy is the NEW
32. Authentic sexy is the NEW
33. Authentic sexy is the NEW
34. Authentic sexy is the NEW

Now, create a story that speaks about your unique expression of authentic sexy by using 5-10 of the authentic sexy definitions that resonated with you from the previous page.

Example (I have bolded the authentic sexy definitions that resonated with me to demonstrate how I have included them within my story): My authentic sexy is my **new confident power** and **route to peace.** This **powerful expression** of sexy helps me step into my **joy** so that I can be an **eruption of deliciousness.** My authentic sexy expresses my **beauty** in **waves of feminine magnificence.** In fact, it's my most powerful **expression of love.**

My authentic sexy is _____

_____

_____

_____

_____

_____

_____

_____

_____

_____

Activation Exercise:

By using activations, such as powerful statement like "I am" linked with whatever you are working to embody, helps your mind and body connect while reprogramming your Truth – almost as if it becomes infused within your DNA.

Below, write your favorite words that describe your authentic sexy.

For example: I am radiant. I am delicious. I am ....

I am: _____

I am: _____

I am: _____

I am: _____

I am: _____

I am: _____

I am: _____

Tips:

1) Activational Truths can help you boost your feelings of beauty, sexiness, worthiness, and more with visual reminders/representations of the Truth.
2) If you are committed to redefining sexy, increasing your confidence and boosting your esteem, say these activation phrases out loud to yourself at least once per day.
3) Better yet, share these activation phrases with your Sexy Sisters and experience the power of someone validating and reflecting back to you your beautiful, authentic self.

Below is the final component of this activity.

Take a pad of sticky notes and write any and all the phrases that resonate with you.

Create at least ten (10) sticky notes for each of your selected phrases and place them in several different places that you will see each day (i.e. your home, office, and vehicle).

These notes will provide you with visual reminders of how delicious you are by infusing the physical spaces you exist in with the Truth.

Every time you see the, say these phrases out loud. (Please note: You are also welcome to create your own).

I am GORGEOUS!

I am worthy of all things good.

I am valuable.

I am incredibly loved.

I deserve to be happy.

Happiness is my birthright.

It is safe for me to be me.

I am vibrant and healthy!

My body does not define me.

I am beautiful inside AND out!

I am lovable.

Sexy is a concept that we, as a culture,
unconsciously give a great deal
of power to.

Redefining sexy to fit your age,
curves, personality and life is a way
to take back the power of sexy so that
you can empower yourself to feel
safe enough to express yourself
and/or sexy in whatever
ways you choose.

Lesson Four:
Time to get NAKED!

It's Time To Strip Away Your Layers,
Remove Your Armor And Stand Up
NAKED, As Gorgeous You.

Wait!

Does this make you a little shy?

Perhaps the concept of being naked (as in seen without all your emotional and psychological armor) is new to you, which may seem a little scary...

Maybe someone in your past told you to put a tent on your circus and stop acting so

S
   I   or playful
     L
        L
            Y
or unabashed
                            or child-like ...

because you are an adult now!!!

Or, Maybe someone told you …

"You are (too) F A T !"

"Too SKINNY!"

"Too T
A
L
"Too
L
SHORT!"
!"

"Your bOObs aren't big enough!"

"You're too O
           L   "You're
           D   too
           !"   SMART!"

         Or,

              "You're
                too
              PRUDE-ish
              for me!"

And it hurt you so much that it

BRUISED YOUR DNA!

Exercise:
Take a minute to think about something*
someone said to you that hurt your
feelings. It can be *anything.*
There is no right or wrong answer here,
my love.

*hint: The first thing that pops into
your head is PERFECT.

HEY
GORGEOUS!

Look over there

Ya, I'm talking to you!

It's cute that you didn't partake in the exercise, but I have to say ...

YOU are the one who opened this book.

YOU are the one who is taking the time (out of your busy life) to play with me!

Even if I wanted to, I cannot do these exercises for you ...

I can *already* do this stuff – which is why I am paying it forward and teaching it to you.

Believe me sister, if you want to REAP the benefits of this book you have to DO THE WORK!

No one can do it for you.

Just reading these words will not be enough.

You need to STEP INSIDE these pages and be an active participant to release your YUM.

Door to
Delciousness
**ENTER
HERE!**

O

If you are thinking, "That's nice, but this stuff doesn't apply to me";

or

"I already know who I am as a sexy being so I don't need to read this";

or

"I am just going to READ the book. I'm not going to DO the exercises. I have no desire to BECOME more connected to my authentic, sexy and playful, human nature."

If these statements reflect your thoughts, as the author of this book experience, I just have to say, with the utmost respect:

I kindly recommend that you close this book IMMEDIATELY and find something else to do with your time.

The truth is, if you don't actively participate in this book, when it's harvest time, meaning when it's time to step into your deliciousness and **dance your life** with your unique sensual groove, you will likely end up exactly where you started - continuing the old habits and patterns that bind you to outdated ways of experiencing your beautiful body and sexy life.

Powerful Truth:
It's normal to feel resistance when the possibility of change presents. For example: if a person has always defined themselves as "not sexy," knowing that *it is possible* for them to be confidently sexy can be a very intimidating thought indeed!

In other words, you have to do the internal work.

My sweet, I want you to be WILDLY successful with the skills and knowledge you gain from this book.

However, I can only give you the tools.

It is up to you to take them for a test drive and discover how to shape them so they can meet your true needs.

Like I have already stated, this book is WAY more than a "how to" book.

The way I see it, you *already are* delicious. You just need a gentle reminder on how to tap into your yum.

These types of exercises are designed to help you UNlearn certain beliefs and/or thought patterns so you can access the Truth of how delicious you already are.

Remember, sexy is not *that* serious AND it is completely accessible to you.

As of right now, I officially give you permission to be sexy for YOU and you alone!

Because authentic sexy comes from the inside.

It's an attitude.

A way of being.

An is-ness that just ...

IS!

Sweetheart, you and I are going in the trenches.

The bogs.

The dark, possibly scary forests of your mind, beliefs, judgments and fears.

Together we are going to open the blinds and invite light into the unconscious crevices of your life, mind, views and actions that are holding you back from your birthright of genuine confidence and joyful expressions of your authentically sexy nature.

Take my hand sweetness.

Jump down the rabbit hole that leads to your version of authentic sexy ...

Your deliciousness is waiting for you!

Let's try this again.

Close your eyes and think about something someone said that hurt your feelings.

The echo of those words can still be heard today – in your actions, feelings, sense of self, etc.

Alright, now I don't want you to focus on that too much. Just hold that remembrance in your head because we are going to work with that shortly.

Real Life Example:

When I was eight years old, my dad sat me down on the steps of our home and said, "Morgan, boys take advantage of girls who are bigger" (if you don't know what I mean, stay with me, it will become clear).

My eight year old mind had *no idea* WHAT he was talking about!

I knew he had previously used the term "big" to describe large (or fat) people. However, I never identified myself as fat.

Startlingly however, it was as though that moment transformed me from a space of child-like innocence, where I *knew* – right down to my DNA – that I was perfect, into a space where I felt like the entire world was judging me.

I believed what my dad said was the truth because children in Canadian society are expected to listen to their parents; what parents say is **gospel.**

In other words, because of what my dad said, I began to believe that the entire world thought I was fat too!

Fear about the repercussions of being fat consumed my 8-year-old mind.

In fact, I can remember wishing that someone would invent a magical machete so I could chop off all of my offending fat! (I really just wanted to be "normal." However, it's scary how "not normal" that thought really is).

The truth is, I am sure my dad's lesson was well intentioned. However, at the core, my dad was teaching me that my feelings of self worth should be completely grounded in my body size and my body should be the barometer I used to discern my social and self worth.

At 8 years of age, I didn't know that my dad was offering me a misguided opinion and lesson in social contexts and viewpoints.

Regardless, the result of my dad's (not-so wise) teachings led me to wage a silent war against my body.

I wrestled with my disappointment in it for not being "perfect."

Essentially, my body had become my WORST enemy.

Powerful Truth:
This sort of body shaming can reinforce the ambiguous status quo around the "perfect" body shape, which can lead to body image issues that can carry on into adult life..

I was "good" and my body was "bad."

This view led me to have no concept of how to *really* see my body.

My meat suit.

The planetary (and temporary) home for my beautiful and loving soul.

Instead, I could only see my body through the lenses my dad gifted me:

> *Be scared of the world because people will hurt you if your body is not perfect.*

At 8, I had no idea what "perfect" meant. I just knew that I was not it. That belief began my cycle of harsh personal self judgment.

Thankfully, a couple of decades later, I began to get bored of judging myself in every minute of every day.

The truth was that regardless of what I did, my body and weight wasn't leading me to happiness, to feeling good about myself or to a partner who respected me, as my dad indicated it would.

Therefore, logic indicated that there must be another route to happiness and safety that was grounded in something *other than* my body. So I opened my mind to the possibilities ...

In doing so, I was gifted with the ability to really *see*.

What I mean by this is: I learned how to see things "as they are" instead of "how they appear to be." See below for an example.

Christopher Columbus & The North American Natives

Christopher Columbus asked the natives to watch for the ships from his homeland so that he would know when they arrived. However, as the story goes, the natives were not able to see the ships until they ran ashore. Why? Because they had never seen a ship before! They had no reference point. They didn't know that *that* (the giant floating thing that was making its way to shore) was the "ship" Mr. Columbus was asking them to watch for.

The theory behind this example is this: if you do not know what you are looking for, how are you going to be able to see it? In other words, your eyes might see something but if your brain can't comprehend or label what your eyes are seeing, it likely won't register. Therefore, it is very important to learn how to *see past* the training you have received thus far in your life so you can see what is *actually* there in front of you.

Before I learned how to really see the world, I journeyed along my path of life blind.

I never questioned the roots of my behavior – what I did and, more importantly, *why I did it.*

Instead, I just lived up to social norms, standards and expectations.

I did what I was told to do and lived my life based on what I was taught was "normal".

Truthfully, I had no idea that questioning what was considered normal was even up for discussion!

Thankfully, after I learned how to SEE, I learned to question everything!

It was because of this questioning that I began to understand that true respect and happiness could never come from outside of me.

In fact, I noticed that the more I respected myself, the more others respected me.

Powerful Truth:
Loving and accepting myself is not an audacious concept but rather my right, as a human being.

The more authentically I showed up in life, the more others liked me.

And, the more I loved myself, the more I *allowed* others to love me.

All of these things brought me happiness, not the size of my body, as my dad indicated it would.

With this new empowered world and body view, I realized I had to let go of my body hate and shame.

Not only was it *not* serving me. It also didn't feel good!

The truth is, I can't blame my dad for his misguided teaching for two reasons:

1) because – even with his flaws, he was always a really good dad,

and

2) deep down I *know* that he was just trying to protect me.

Besides, it's because of this experience that I have something to share here with you ...

I have shared this very personal story with you because I am sure my dad, just like whoever said that horrible thing that hurt you, *never intended* for it to impact you the way it did.

In fact, I bet that if that person knew how much hurt their words caused you they would take them back instantly!

I bet they would even say, "I'm sorry."

Alright, YOUR turn, Beautiful!

I know you have a story too ...

What did someone, somewhere say to you that is keeping you stuck?

What unkindness continues to spin in your head?

Do you know that this unkindness is a lie?

Do you know that you are actually perfect?

This is the Truth, my sweet.

What aspects of your life have you built around the unconscious "lies" and misguided realities you have been taught to view as REALity?

Are the serving you? Or have they become as useless as broken records?

Can you entertain the idea of giving yourself permission to just let them go?

I am personally giving you permission, sweetness …

Let go of anything that someone told you that has crushed your heart, stunted your flourishing life and/or bruised your gentle and beautiful soul.

Let go of what is not serving you, Beautiful.

It is
no longer
your burden
to carry.

Let go and take a breath. (Five slow inhales and five slow exhales).
Sit with the space you are creating.
You have nowhere to be right now but here with me on this page.

Coaching Q & A
(Circle your choice)

1) Can you accept the possibility of letting go of your past hurts?

      YES   or,   YES

2) Are you open to exploring a new way of being?

      YES   or,   YES

3) *Is it possible* that if you let go of something that both doesn't feel good to you and is no longer working for you, something delicious just may fill the space?

      YES   or,   YES

4) Is it possible for you to sit with wonder as you create space for a new way of being to set in?

      YES   or,   YES

5) Is it possible for you to write your past hurt on the following page, rip it out of this book, then tear it into a million pieces, burn it, shred it, and/or flush it down the toilet?

      YES   or,   YES

Please note:
I only put "YES" as an option for three reasons:

1) I am asking if it is possible. And I am pretty sure anything is possible.

2) Has saying NO been working for you?

3) YES is the key to change. Sometimes your monkey mind (your ego) says NO so you can stay in your familiar stuckness.

In other words, by saying YES you create the space to *activate* change in your delicious life.

Past Hurt Page:

Directions:

1) Write past hurt (or hurts) on this page.

2) Rip this page out of this book and do whatever you want with it (tear it, shred it, flush it and/or burn it). That's right, Beautiful. I am giving you permission. (I bet it will be VERY therapeutic for you!)

By the way, if you need a hug or a tissue, here you go.

I love you.

When you are ready, turn the page and keep reading.

New Positive Frame Page:
Now that we have gotten rid of the old and yucky –
let's find the positive and delicious!

Directions:
1) Take a lined piece of paper and count out 100 lines.

2) In ONE sitting write 100 things you like about yourself on the page(s).* (This exercise takes between 5-20 minutes).

3) Now, look at all the amazing things you like about you. Chose 10-20 of your favorites and write a few sentences about who you are – according to you. It's important that the sentences reflect you. Therefore, use your own terms and your own words.

For Example:
I am a beautiful, vibrant woman who radiates love, peace and acceptance. I live my life to the fullest – defining for myself who I am. I am my biggest cheerleader and most loyal fan. I am lovable, gorgeous, sexy and sassy. I am valuable, delicious and worthy of all things good. I love me. I am amazing!

4) Refer to this expression of you – your new frame – whenever you need a reminder of how incredible and yummy you are.

*Keep these pages somewhere you can refer to them regularly and remind you of your amazing deliciousness.

Positive Statements About ME!
(directions on the previous page).

Lesson Five:
You are beautiful.

---

*Feelings Of Esteem And Worth
Are Inside Jobs.*

There are lots of ideas about what beautiful means.

I am not interested in those.

I am interested in what beautiful *feels like* to you.

Below is an exercise designed to help you do just that; discover for yourself what beautiful *feels like* to you – in your own way and on your own terms.

In other words, goodbye socially prescribed definitions of beautiful and hello personal, joyful, and authentic experience!

Exercise: Finding Authentic Beauty

Bring your awareness to this moment. There is no "right" or "wrong" way to do this.

Feel your bum in your seat. Take a deep breath and feel your belly expand as you draw breath in.

Suspend judgment.

Be here now.

Take a few more breaths and when you are ready, bring your awareness to the part of yourself from where you experience expressions of love.

Rest in this space and take five deep breaths.

When you are ready, expand this space and acknowledge the JOY that lives here.

Feel the lightness, the sparkle.

Underline this feeling with compassion and femininity.

This is what I mean by beautiful.

True beauty is not "serious."

It's not complicated.

It's also not something someone taught you, as in an ego based expression or image of something.

It's actually a feeling. A lightness. An essence. An *experience* that is unique to you.

And, the bonus is that you can't get it wrong!

From now on, anytime you forget that you are incredibly beautiful, do this exercise to remember how exquisite you are!

Lesson Six:
You hold the pen.
Draw the portrait of your
most delicious life.

---

*Find The Courage To Live Your Most
Delicious Life. No One Else Can
Do It For You.*

T he truth is that you are the only one who can live your life.

It sounds simple, because it is.

The responsibility for *you* living a delicious life rests solely upon your shoulders because you are the only person who knows - right down to a DNA/cellular level - what incredible gifts you bring to the world.

In other words, because you are the only person who has the capability to see your best life, you have to live *your life* on *your own terms.*

And in order to do this, you have to gain clarity on what really, truly matters to you.

In other words, you have to be able SEE you in order to fully EM-BRACE you; to fully HONOR you and EMBODY *your* unique and unrepeatable greatness.

The truth is, when you acknowledge and celebrate your (you)nique and authentic gifts, the external validation you used to seek will become obsolete.

In fact, living your life for someone else or on someone else's terms will no longer serve you because you will be able to recognize your amazing contribution to this planet*, which will help you stand tall in new levels of confidence and personal power.
(*Hint: it's when you live your **heart song**.)

The following exercise will help you uncover how your authentic self desires to express life.

This clarity will make it easier for you to let go of what *isn't* serving you, while illuminating the path to your most delicious life; the path where the woman who embodies your authentic sexy lives.

She may be a woman you know.

Or, she may be a woman you are going to get to know!

Either way ... let's find out!

Exercise:
Imagine that you are very close to the end of your life[1]. You have a few, short days left on this planet. From that vantage point, identify what is most significant to you. Create a list of the five distinguishing elements that standout as being paramount to your end-of-life self in order for you to feel at peace with saying goodbye to your time on this planet. In other words, what specific qualities do you need to live in order to experience your most delicious life?

---

1 More than a decade of personal development work (and professional training) has repeatedly shown that the best way to get clear on what is important to an individual is for them to examine their life from a mortality perspective. This exercise is my version of a death-bed perspective.

Maybe kindness is important to you.

Generosity.

Love.

Maybe it's important that you chose to LIVE every day of your beautiful life instead of being too scared to taste the delicious experiences life brought to the table.

Maybe you want to be remembered for your friendliness or attentiveness; that you were the most compassionate person you knew; or that you lived your life honoring joy, passion, beauty, and determination.

There is no right or wrong way to answer this, my love.

What ways to express and animate your life are the most important to you?

What are the qualities that your end-of-life self knows were important for her to embody so she could lie on her death bed *knowing* that she led a fantastic and unsquandered life?

Take a minute to write out your thoughts below.
1)

2)

3)

4)

5)

I am going to take a WILD guess and say that chances are your end of life self really doesn't care that you were (or weren't) the sexiest/youngest looking/most beautiful woman who ever lived on planet earth.

She understands that beauty is culturally determined and looks are truly only skin deep.

She knows very well that with time, skin gets wrinkly; external beauty fades.

I bet she also knows that whatever has animated her -- her unique light and authentic way of being -- still exists within her, even in her last few days of life.

Now, let's ground this exercise and frame it within the context of your life. Take each of your traits and put one in each of the available spaces in the graph below.

Your Traits	Confident	Authentic	Free*					
How Often?								
Everyday								
3 days/wk								
Every week								
Every 2 wks								
Every month								
Every 3 mon.								
Every 6 mon.								
Every year								
Never								

*Free refers to being able to live your life on your terms.

Now color in how much or how little you experience each unique aspect in your life, as indicated on the graph.

For example: If you experience it often, then you will color in all the spaces from the bottom "Never" to the top "Everyday." However, if you only experience that expression every three months, then you would only color in the spaces from "Every 3 months" down.

What does your graph look like?

Does is show balance?

Ideally, you want to have a full chart, which represents a full, balanced life.

Why Is This Exercise Important?

1. Gaining clarity about what your most delicious life looks like – as defined by you – shows you what *actually is* versus what you want. This exercise allows you to make adjustments because it shows you where you need to take action.

2. Many people are visual learners, thus it serves them greatly to see where there is a lack of juiciness and/or balance in their life. By seeing a visual representation, they can start appreciating what they need to change in order to enhance deliciousness and to bring their life into alignment with what truly matters to them.

3. The concepts of "authentic", "confident" (synonymous in this context with sexy and beautiful), and "free" are aspects of your in-credible woman-ness that sometimes gets lost in the noise of adult life. I added these into the graph because they are pillars of the lessons in this book experience.

I will ask you this again.

WHO do you want to be remembered as?

What is it that REALLY matters to you?

Will your life be juicy if you continue to hide, stand in your way, or allow other's views to shape *your* life?

Or, will you work to make your future self proud by living her heart song boldly?

Remember, her heart song is your heart song, my love.

Looking back from this vantage point, can you see the steps you need to take in order to create that life?

What choices do you need to make?

What actions do you have to live?

What Truths do you have to speak in order to make this your reality?

What steps can you take – today, tomorrow, and for the rest of your days – that will move you closer to your most joyful, vibrant and sexy life, as defined by you?

For example: workout, live unabashedly, hug someone you love, say YES! to only what you really want, refuse to let your dreams die inside of you, give yourself the gift of you time, or live boldly as you so you can inspire others to live boldly as them.

Take some time to reflect and write this out on the following page.

Action steps I can take today:

Action steps I can take this week:

Action steps I can take this month:

Action steps I can take this year:

Small but consistent daily actions will move you
forward into your best life; a delicious life that is not
only nourishing and fulfilling but also designed by you.

Powerful Thought:
The Death Bed Test (DBT)

To help you ground the concept of consistently moving towards living your best life, put everything to the DBT.

Specifically, ask yourself if the activities you are choosing to fill your days with are things you would do if you only had two (2) months left to live.

If not, it did not pass the DBT and it is really not *that* important.

Lesson Seven:
Love and acceptance starts from within.

It's Your Human Right To Experience Love.
TRUE LOVE Exists Inside Of You.
However, It Is Up To You To Tap Into It's
Abundant Flow.

My sweet, darling friend, I ask you this:

Are you ready to get out of your own way and live like no one is watching (or judging) you?

Are you ready to love yourself (and your body) BOLDLY?

Are you ready to UNlearn all those silly ideas that have been rolling around in your head that make you feel less than delicious?

(You know, the ones that say, "I can't be sexy. I'm a mom." "I'm too fat to be sexy!" "I'm shy. I could never be sexy." "I'm too old to be sexy!" and blah, blah, blah).

YES!

That's right!

It's time to STOP World War III on your beautiful body.

It's time to START remembering that you are entitled to living a delicious human experience.

After all, being HUMAN is your birthright, my sweet.

Your destiny on this incredible planet earth.

And, why mess with destiny?

The truth is, not loving yourself is POWERFUL (and deflating).

However, if you choose, those days can finally be behind you.

The next exercise is designed to physically move you into the space of your unique expression of authentic sexy.

By engaging this type of learning modality (kinesthetic), you are giving yourself the opportunity to experience – through your movements – what triggers you to feel confident, shy, ridiculous, happy and more.

By being aware of how you feel when you start expressing your authentic sexy via movement, other areas/beliefs/thought patterns/ etc. that you still have to UNlearn will surface.

By knowing what you need to UNlearn and/or reprogram, you will be able to continue to evolve into an even more radiant expression of authentic, sexy you ... which is so delicious!

Example:

I was attending a Groove Method[1] dance class a few years ago and was instructed to "walk in time with the music, hurriedly, as if going to work."

I did as I was told and had a powerful "Ah-ha!" moment. I realized that my expression of "going to work" combined severe and hurried body movements with a stern facial expression.

The "Ah-ha!" occurred because I actually LIKE working, even though my facial expression and movements indicated that my view of work is serious and void of joy.

It was due to that exercise that I gained wisdom and clarity around ways I express myself that are inauthentic to my actual views, which proved to be so powerful because that knowledge allowed me to reprogram my body language to match and express my authentic beliefs.

Exercise:
Pretend you are a model in a high profile photo shoot.

Your FAVORITE magazine has asked you to be on the cover.

Now, put this book down and strike a pose.

Any pose you like.

Obviously, I want to see some FLAVA!

FLAVA = fancy, laughable, awesome, vigorous & audacious!

Pose for the camera!

Sell it
to me,
Gorgeous!

OK, for some reason, I see we are back to where we were a few lessons ago.

Are you feeling shy?

Or, are you wondering how pretending to be a model in a high profile photo shoot equates with self love?

If you are wondering about the latter, the answer is this:

Many women have inhibitions about being bold.

Being playful.

Shining their light and being authentically confident.

Self love doesn't have to manifest via granola munching, eyes-closed-swaying, positive affirmation singing behaviors.

Those methods have their place. However, *this method* encourages you to get up and out of your comfort zone to PLAY! (I don't know about you but 9 times out of 10, I opt for the fun, slightly wacky and completely joy filled option).

Powerful Truth:

Many women secretly wish they *could* do a photo shoot for their favorite magazine (be it for cooking, fashion, fitness, golf, etc.). However, most hide their desire under a cloak of "shyness."
This type of exercise offers excellent insight into how *free* they allow themselves to be.
Specifically, because how they do this exercise is an excellent reflection of how they do everything in their lives - boldly or they just imagine doing it.

And, if you are worried about being "perfect" in this photo shoot, please relax.

Not only does perfect not exist, but this is not a "REAL" photo shoot!

We're just playing a game.

Besides ... WHO IS GOING TO SEE YOU DO THIS?!?

WHY are you being shy?

What is the *worst* that could happen if you did this exercise?

I'll tell you ...

YOU

COULD

DIE!

Seriously?

Please remember, sweetness: you can't get this wrong!

This "shy self" is a mask you hide behind.

It is not YOU and therefore is not delicious.

Remember, I can see you. Your heart is SO BEAUTIFUL! Please let it shine so everyone else in your life can see it too.

Let's try this again …

Aaaaaaannnndd, ACTION!

POSE FOR THE CAMERA GORGEOUS!

Show me your MEOW!

(I am not entirely sure what that means, but I am sure you can figure out how to do it).

Seriously.

Get out of your chair.

Shake off your shy

and DO THIS!

YOU'RE GOING ON THE COVER OF

(insert the name of your favorite magazine),

BABY!

Great work!

I am SO PROUD of you!

How did that feel?

You took a little risk and totally nailed it!

*High five!

NOTES

1 Misty Tripoli
http://www.mistytripoli.com
http://theworldgroovemovement.com

Lesson Eight:
(E)sensual self care

*Engaging In (E)sensual Self Care Is A
Powerful Method To Help You Feel
Incredibly Nurtured And Ultra Sexy.*

O n the following page is a list for you to fill in with activities you LOVE to do. The activities you list *must* be "treats" (things or activities that you do not typically allow yourself to indulge in).

When you finish the list, please show it to someone and tell them that you are committing to doing TWO (2) of these self care activities each week.

Sign the commitment note at the bottom of the page and have your witness sign it as well.

Remember that feeling good starts from within.
When you build time into your busy life to do the nourishing
and delicious things that make you happy, you are taking
care of yourself. These actions of (e)sensual self care are
extremely necessary because they ensure that your
needs are being taken care of.
Doing these things also fills you up emotionally so that you
have more love and kindness to give to others.

(E)Sensual Self Care:
A List Of Things You LOVE To Do:

1.
2.
3.
4.
5.
6.
7.
8.
9.
10.
11.
12.
13.
14.
15.
16.
17.
18.
19.
20.
21.
22.
23.

I _____promise
to schedule one (1) of these delicious exercises into my week EACH
week.

_____

Signed (your name)   Today's date

_____

Signed (witness)   Today's date

Lesson Nine:
Sexy ... it's not that serious.

Sexy Is An Innate Aspect Of Your Being.

When you understand the importance of redefining sexy, you open yourself up to take action.

When you redefine sexy to fit your age, curves, personality and life, sexy becomes accessible – regardless of *who* you thought you were and *what* you thought your limitations were before engaging this book experience.

In an effort to solidify the realities of: 1) authentic sexy and 2) sexy not being *that* serious, the following exercise will help infuse these delicious Truths into your DNA.

Remember: you CANNOT not get authentic sexy right!

Exercise:
Make a triple chin and stick out your belly and bum as far as they will go. Pretend that you just got off of a giant elephant and your legs have not regained their ability to straighten completely. Walk around the room like this and say, "I'M SEXY!" as loud as you can. Say it 25 times.
Say it like you mean it.

How was that?

Did you feel SILLY?!?

(Ha ha ha! I sure HOPE so, or you weren't doing it right! Wink!)

"OW! I feel good!" *James Brown[1]*

Isn't it interesting how after about 10 or 15 times of you saying, "I'M SEXY," even while you looked pretty darn funny, you started to really "get" how NOT serious sexy is?!?

Are you starting to understand how FUN and delicious it is to just LET GO, PLAY and BE?

Even more than that, are you starting to understand how beautiful you are?

On the inside AND on the outside?

EVEN IF you have never before identified yourself as beautiful and/or sexy before!

The fact of the matter is this: it *really* doesn't matter what you look like (via playful actions, clothes, makeup, etc.) on the outside because ...

Sexy is not *that* serious.

NOTES

1 Brown, J. (singer). (1994). I feel good [Song from the album Turn it Loose]. Drive Archive.

"You CANNOT not get authentic sexy right!"

Conclusion & Sexy Sisterhood™ Induction

I want to remind you that you are welcome and encouraged to re-read and/or re-do any and all of the exercises in this book.

There is also the Sexy … it's not that serious™ workbook and online course for those interested in diving deeper in facilitated UNlearning and reprogramming.

As you begin to redefine sexy to fit your age, curves, personality and life, your expression of authentic sexy will also grow and evolve.

Additionally, reconnecting with and expanding upon your personal definition of authentic sexy will ensure that you continue moving on a positive and healthy trajectory.

With that, thank you for sharing your incredible light with me.

You are so authentically sexy!

To acknowledge all the hard work, UNlearning, DEprogramming, learning and REprogramming you've done within this book experience, I would like to personally welcome you into the Global Chapter of the Sexy Sisterhood™ Movement!

On page 183 is your induction pledge.

Please fill it in and then read it out loud.

And know that I am so happy to have you in the Sisterhood!

You bring so much to our movement.

You are delicious, unrepeatable and irresistibly sexy.

THANK YOU FOR BEING YOU!

Until we meet again – stay Authentically Sexy!

Love,

Morgan

I _____ promise to take
responsibility for my SEXY.

Because I love me,

I AM sexy and I know I ROCK!

From now on I choose to share my awesome deliciousness with the
world because I CAN and because I know that if I don't I would be
robbing the world of my incredible light.

I understand that I am unrepeatable.

I am delicious.

I am a miracle of sexy.

And it is up to ME to love and accept myself first.

I relinquish the desire to be in competition with other women because they are my sisters and they are sexy in their own right.

Finally, I know that I deserve the best life possible, so I am going to
live my AUTHENTIC SEXY in my own way and on
my own terms, *anywhere* I choose, in ways that nourish and uplift
me.

With this I welcome more JOY, CONFIDENCE, VIBRANCY,
SUCCESS and better RELATIONSHIPS in my life!

I am a SEXY SISTER!

_____

Please sign your name and date it.

Trusted Resources Section

---

*Additional Support To Help You Embody The Most
Delicious Expression Of Gorgeous You!*

---

3 **NEW** Books In The
Sexy ... it's not *that* serious Series!

• A Cancer Survivor's Guide To Feeling Beautiful, Confident & Sexy Again

• A Health Care Professionals Guide To Understanding The Importance of Sexy, Beauty and Body Image In Post Cancer Patient Care

• Helping Your Loved One Feel Sexy After They've Experienced Cancer

Launching OCTOBER, 2013
For Breast Cancer Month

For More Information Or To PRE-ORDER Your Copies:
WWW.HOWTOBESEXY.TV

Use code
'Sexy' for
$100 off one
of our weekend
trainings

Are you...

- ready to stand tall as the beautiful, incredible woman you always knew you could be?
- plagued by negative self talk in your head every day?
- Ready to embrace the new, sexier, healthier version of you?

Join us...

for a weekend 'tool-kit' training designed to empower the real you;

- Embrace your most successful and passionate life
- Create your future...on purpose and transform your past
- Embrace you authentic sexy through passionately living your most successful life.

Use all of this and more to create greater wealth, health, and happiness in your life... *now*

Find out more...

By web: www.ChooseRESULTS.ca

By Email: KKessler@ChooseRESULTS.ca

By Phone: 647.343.0664

Are You Ready To ...

- Bust through your beauty blocks?
- Feel your incredible value and worth like never before?
- Learn how to feel beautiful, confident and sexy today?

If so ... it's time to take the challenge!

WWW.21DAYBEAUTYBREAKTHROUGH. COM

ORDER TODAY
& save 50% off the regular price!
(save over $98!)

PLUS! Get over $1347 in Bonuses!
Promo Code: "BREAKTHROUGH"

WWW.21DAYBEAUTYBREAKTHROUGH. COM

ACTIVATE *YOUR* 50 SHADES OF SEXY!

Inspiration for Transformation
"Live Your Sexiest, Most Turned on Life"

50 Positive Activation Cards To Inspire Transformation

Learn how to live your sexiest, most turned on life in ways that honor YOU: your age, curves, personality and life. Choose a card each week, each day or each time you are seeking guidance to uncover the next step on your authentic sexy journey. Reflect and act on these concepts and your delicious life will be painted with 50 Shades of Sexy!

SPECIAL PROMOTION:
Save 50% off the retail price!
(save over $8.75!)
Promo Code: "TRANSFORMATION"

Order today:

WWW.HOWTOBESEXY.TV

VIP & GROUP COACHING

You're on the cusp of a serious breakthrough. You're ready to feel confident, vibrant, happy and sexy, in your own ways and on your own terms ... but you haven't figured out how to get there.

Fret not, Gorgeous ... I know the way.

VIP and/or GROUP coaching is for you:
- if you're not at peace in your body,
- if you wrestle with never feeling quite "good enough",
- if you feel invisible and yearn to be seen,
- if you are unhappy in your life and searching for answers,
- if you are terrified to let go of what's familiar but want to experience what else is available to you (the relationship you've been craving, the professional success you desire, or finding the courage to live your sexiest, most turned on life).

If this sounds like you, then I invite you to say YES! to your Dreams, your Femininity, and your Authentic Sexy by taking action and joining me in one of my powerful coaching programs.

It's your time. You deserve to feel exquistely delicious!

SPECIAL PROMOTION*:
Save 25% off all coaching packages!

Promo Code: "COACHING"
All promo orders will receive over $1537 in BONUSES!

Space Is Limited. Register Today:

WWW.HOWTOBESEXY.TV